W

*"Light, funny and very informative.
Definitely wins a space in my
library."*

> Perry Deshler, Owner
> A Bargain in Books
> Second Generation NATIVE

*"Thoroughly enjoyed the book.
Brought back lots of memories and
many a chuckle!! I recommend it."*

> Nita Hastings,
> Second Generation NATIVE

"Every state should have one."

> Dick O'Neill,
> ALIEN from Florida

Disclaimer

About the Author:

Linda Murdock, moved to Denver from the Midwest in 1982, working at jobs that qualified her to write about Colorado. She started as a stockbroker during the oil bust, worked for a railroad and a gold mining company and has owned her own business since 1989. She is an avid history and genealogy buff. You might see her on warm days running around Denver on her little blue scooter.

Her first book, *A Busy Cook's Guide to Spices*, shows how to flavor foods in a practical way. Organized by what we eat, such as corn, potatoes, beef, salads, etc., she lists the spices and recipes under that particular food.

ALMOST NATIVE
HOW TO PASS AS A COLORADAN

by
Linda Murdock

[signature]

BELLWETHER BOOKS
Denver, Colorado

Cover Illustration by Mike Motz
Cover Design by Scott O'Neill

Also by Linda Murdock
A Busy Cook's Guide to Spices, How to
Introduce New Flavors to Everyday Meals

To order, contact:
Bellwether Books
P O Box 9757
Denver, CO 80209
murd@bellwetherbooks.com
1-800-924-6488

ISBN: 0-9704285-2-9
LCCN: 2004093479

Murdock, Linda.
Almost native how to pass as a Coloradan
/ Linda Murdock
Denver, Colo. : Bellwether Books, c2004
128 p. ill. ;
ISBN: 0-9704285-2-9

10 9 8 7 6 5 4 3 2 1
Printed in the United States of America

Dedication
to Dick,
for Scott,
his semi-NATIVE son

From a 1909 Denver and Rio Grande
Railroad brochure:

One reason the west has prospered
is that the weak, the timid,
the hesitating, the doubtful,
the suspicious
have always stayed at home,
while the brave, the resolute and
determined have struck out
when opportunities beckoned.

Acknowledgements

Thanks to Dave Gonzales, who keeps me focused. He lets me discover my own creativity. His encouragement and advice mean more than he knows. Thanks to Barbara Osgood-Hartness for her organization, editing and friendship skills. She brings calm to the frenzied, humility to the self-assured. Thanks to Perry Deshler at A Bargain In Books in Englewood. He lent me several key books on Colorado and made mine richer as a result. Thanks to the Denver Public Library, especially the helpful reference staff and Western History Department. The Colorado Historical Society keeps me informed about the state. The Colorado Railroad Museum library had immediate answers to all questions. Others helped or guided me with census, health and Vietnam data–Joyce Ayoub, Patricia V. Dickerson and Daniel R. Law. Thanks to all the readers whether NATIVE, SEMI-NATIVE or ALIEN. You know who you are–Scott, "Dad," Nita, Jan, Perry, Jim Bell, Tom King, owner of Denver's Queen Anne Bed & Breakfast and Abbott Fay. All took the time to carefully critique the work.

Book titles that didn't make the cut:

The Colorado Casserole, Mixing up a Native

The Counterfeit Coloradan, How to Pass as a Native

The Home Grown Coloradan, How to Pick a Native

Desperately Seeking Natives

The Native Coloradan, Living in a Heightened State

Pass as a Native, Stay as a Coloradan

Native Fad, Colorado Pad

When in Colorado, Do as the Natives Do

I'm Coloradan, I'm Native & By Gosh People Like Me

Table of Contents

Maps & . . .

Gray Matter

Introduction

Why would anyone decide to move to Colorado? Why do we move anywhere? We come for job opportunities or because of a job transfer. We come because a family member or friend moved here and convinced us to move here, too. Specifically we come because we like mountains, nature and skiing.

But for a Midwesterner like me, the attraction to Colorado, particularly Denver, was the slower-than-most-cities pace (not so true any more), the feeling I could walk around safely and the friendliness of the people. The tourist propaganda that promised 300 days of sunshine a year was also seductive. (The truth is any day with at least forty-five minutes of sunshine is included in that count.)

The fact that the average age of Mile High residents, when I came to Denver in 1982, was thirty something and that there were more single males than females, was a definite plus. Yes, I landed one, even though it took four years.

Back then it was commonplace to be served in a Colorado restaurant (especially in Boulder) by someone with more degrees than a thermometer. One person in four had a college education, and there was and still is a tangible sense of independence, that suits an entrepreneurial spirit such as mine.

There are many new things to learn about living in Colorado. It means layering your clothes and practicing the boy scout motto of "always being prepared," for the weather, that is. It also means expanding your vocabulary with new terminology, such as chinook winds and verga, hogback and Continental Divide. And living high requires new accessories, such as sunblock, Carmex®, sunglasses and a full water bottle.

Here then is the wonderful world of Colorado presented in what I hope is an amusing and enlightening, albeit tongue-in-cheek, way. This book will give you the insights necessary to pass as a genuine NATIVE. Whether you are contemplating a move, know someone who lives here, are a new transplant, or, as a NATIVE, you just want to have a chuckle at the expense of these tenderfoots, I hope you will enjoy this informative introduction to the not-so-wild West. About the only thing wrong with this state is that new people keep moving here! Hopefully, this will make you feel like one of us, whether you decide to stay or just visit awhile.

NATIVE Origins

In November 1978 Robert
Shaver of Boulder started a fad that
soon appeared on bumper stickers
all over Colorado. He started the
Colorado Native Society. For eighteen dollars a year and an affidavit
saying you were born in Colorado,
you could join. With your membership you got a certificate, T-shirt,
decal and a subscription to
Colorado Native News.

Shaver claimed that historic
preservation and the environment
were his major concerns given the
crush of newcomers to the state.
Although he hoped it would become
a political force, it did not and even
Shaver eventually dropped his
membership.

The NATIVE bumper sticker
craze that followed was his biggest
impact. Back in 1960 Bill Condit
had designed Colorado's automobile
license plates for a measly forty-five
dollars. Shaver used the reverse of
this green mountain silhouette, but
instead of the usual numbers and
letters, he put the single word:

Soon it seemed as if everyone had a
sticker. Newcomers and NATIVES
alike reacted with variations, such as:

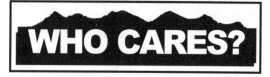

There was even a T-shirt for babies with the insignia NEW NATIVE.

Eric Glade, a non-NATIVE from Utah, trademarked a version and sold over 75,000 bumper stickers. Today companies are still making variations of the stickers often putting in town names. The state updated its license plate design recently to reflect a more accurate skyline, adding shadows to make the mountains look more three-dimensional. Today the NATIVE, like the original bumper sticker is getting harder and harder to find.

Where Ya From?

When asked this, never admit to being a Texan or, what we affectionately refer to as, a Californicator. After all, you Golden Staters have been drinking our water for years. You may as well come and see its mountainous source. It is much better to say you are Canadian, from the Midwest or even the Northwest. NATIVES do not have accents. So if you think you hear one, it is probably coming from you.

Don't honk your horn, if you're from California

In the 1990's most of the newly non-NATIVES came from California. There were so many (150,000) that they thought of renaming the area from Fort Collins to Colorado Springs Dos Angeles and comically referred to the state as Sprawlorado. NATIVES were not amused.

If you're from Austin, Texas or California, you might prefer living in Boulder, the land of the free-for-all and home of the Buffaloes (the foot-ball team of the University of Colorado). The hometown of astro-naut Scott Carpenter and Mork from Ork tends to be a little spacey. Vegetarians, herbalists and meta-physicists are welcome. In the land of Boulder if you're dizzy from the altitude, few there will notice.

If you're a Texan, you have the advantage of already owning a pair of boots. Just get rid of that Texas license plate, before anyone sees it. The cowboy hat and gun rack still work, but seem better suited in towns with names like Rifle or Gunbarrel. It is acceptable to keep the pickup, but a big-honking SUV is more acceptable to urban NATIVES. (If you're going to drive a Hummer you may as well keep the Texas plates, because we already know where you came from.)

Bible belters, teetotalers and military folk feel right at home in conservative Colorado Springs. They put the "fun" back into fundamental-ism. The Springs used to be one of the cheesiest tourist draws in the West. Sadly, attractions like the Hall of President's Wax Museum, which melted into oblivion, the Woodcarver's Museum and the old Clock Museum are no more. At least Santa's Workshop survived. Those of you new to the area can relate to this tackiness, if you've ever been to Gatlinburg, Tennessee or Wall Drugs in South Dakota. In spite of all this, the Pike's Peak scenery of the Springs attracts a lot of newcomers.

Denver is the island capital of our vast semiarid, land-locked state of Colorado. There isn't a city of equal size for 500 miles in any direc-tion. So consider yourself a voluntary immigrant and enjoy the beauty. It's unlikely you'll ever hear a NATIVE say, "Too bad you had to leave ____, it is so much prettier there."

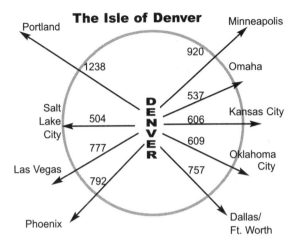

The Isle of Denver

We're proud of our beautiful surroundings. While non-NATIVES refer to Colorado as the Switzerland of America, NATIVES are more likely to say that Switzerland is the Colorado of Europe.

CALLING ALL AREA CODES

Denver Metro	**303, 720**
Bailey	Georgetown
Boulder	Idaho Springs
Castle Rock	Longmont
Evergreen	Parker

South/East Colorado	**719**
Alamosa	Pueblo
Cañon City	Rocky Ford
Colorado Springs	Trinidad

North/West Colorado	**970**
Aspen	Greeley
Durango	Grand Junction
Estes Park	Gunnison
Fort Collins	Steamboat Springs
Fort Morgan	Sterling
Glenwood Springs	Vail

Why so Dizzy?

While a NATIVE craves an espresso, a non-NATIVE is more likely to demand oxygen. It is all in your altitude. If you are toasting your new home, you'll find that it costs less to get drunk here. Take it easy on the alcohol. You can drink less, while feeling the effects more.

After all, you are a mile closer to the sun. Consider drinking that other beverage–water. Take it easy the first few days. Do not be concerned unless you are still huffing and puffing after the first week. Then you are either ill, terribly out of shape or having a religious experience.

Symptoms of altitude sickness include nausea, headaches, dizziness and irregular sleep patterns. Your sweat evaporates, so you do not realize you are dehydrated. Carry around a full water bottle wherever you go. You'll thank me later.

NO BULL

Livestock is also susceptible to altitude sickness. It is known as brisket disease in cattle. These cattle are "cured" when transported to lower elevations. They are not allowed to breed, though, to avoid passing along the trait. The most tested humans for the effects of altitude live in Leadville at 10,188 feet.

Here's a neat bonus: You can take a shower or go swimming at night and both your towel and swimsuit are dry by morning. Try that in Atlanta! That should prove to you just how dry it is around here.

Become familiar with these products: sunblock, sunscreen, sunglasses, suncerely! Skin cancer is no fun, but you are like a sitting duck in Colorado with its high altitude and numerous cloud-free days.

One amusing side effect of the increased elevation is the decreased air pressure. The change in sea level, which causes potato chip bags to swell, also causes you to pass more gas. None have shown the courage for further study, since few are willing to admit to this phenomenon.

One good thing about living a Mile High happens when you go visit friends and relatives out of state. Breathing is so much easier *down there*, you end up impressing everyone with your stamina.

ONE MILE HIGH

The touristy thing to do is to visit the state capitol building in Denver and get your picture taken on whichever step is currently marked at 5280 feet—a mile high.

Where in Colorado?

Front Range, Foothills, Eastern Slope, etc. These are just a few of the NATIVE geographic terms, you should learn before exploring the state or trying to figure out the regional weather forecasts and traffic reports.

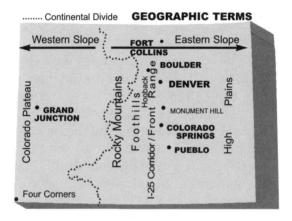

.... Continental Divide **GEOGRAPHIC TERMS**

The **Front Range** means different things to different people. Most of the time it includes Fort Collins south to Denver and Colorado Springs. It is the most heavily populated region of the state in front of, that is, east of the Rocky Mountains. It is also referred to as the **I-25 Corridor**, in which case it may include Pueblo. A broader term for Front Range would be **Eastern Slope**, which includes all the cities mentioned, plus any area east of the Rockies.

Denver actually lies in a pocket between the mountains and the **High Plains** to the east. This helps create that lovely brown cloud of scum (inversion layer) that you see hanging over the city from a distance.

The **Hogback** runs approximately north and south just west of Denver near Morrison. You drive right through it on southbound 285 near I-70. These huge, uplifted rock formations look like rounded humps. Do not confuse these with the **Flatirons** in Boulder, also rocky outcroppings, but jagged, not round and naked of greenery.

The **Foothills** lie east of the Rockies, but west of Denver and the Hogback. These Foothills, if located in Tennessee, would be called the Smokey Mountains. In Colorado since the Foothills are smaller and totally covered with conifers (that is evergreens or Christmas-looking trees) they only rate the sissy designation of "hills."

The **Fourteeners** are mountains over 14,000 feet above sea level. They and other peaks lie along the backbone of the state or what we call the **Continental Divide**. This divide determines the *natural* direction of the rivers on the continent, thus its name. Rivers east of this line, including the South Platte, Rio Grande and Arkansas flow to the Atlantic Ocean or Gulf of Mexico. Rivers west, including the Colorado, the Dolores, Gunnison and Yampa/Green flow to the Pacific Ocean.

TAKE A PEAK

Colorado has between fifty-two and fifty-seven Fourteeners (depending on your definition) and about 1100 peaks over 10,000 feet high. If I can climb a Fourteener, so can you. The hardest parts are: getting up before the sun so you can get down before the lightning; lugging up a gallon of water and other necessary gear; climbing in slow motion as other hikers scurry past; and trying not to sound like a mule, hee-hawing for oxygen all the way to the top.

Although rivers here appear puny, rafting them is a big attraction. Beginning as mountain snow melt, rivers drain downhill and expand as they settle onto flatter ground like Kansas. Rocks lie so near the surface that water has nothing to soak into and flash floods are a real concern. Climb to higher ground if you are caught in a storm. Try not to snicker when you see a river that would barely pass as a stream in the Midwest.

RIVER MAP

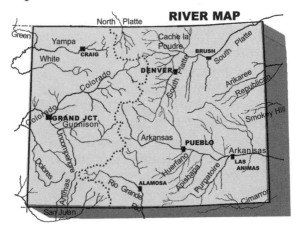

The **Eisenhower Tunnel** is located on I-70 at the Continental Divide. There, a strategically-placed internet camera, shows the divide's weather conditions. It lets truckers know if it's safe to continue west from Denver, and lets skiers know if it's safe to proceed to the nearest ski resort. The full name of the tunnel, Eisenhower-Johnson, is seldom used.

13,817 FOOT FOLKLORE

An almost fourteener near Fairplay was named after a ballroom dancer with fancy shoes. She nursed many miners during the smallpox epidemic of 1863. When the survivors went to thank her with a bag of money, she had disappeared. The mountain is called Mt. Silverheels.

The **Western Slope**, also known as the **Colorado Plateau**, refers to most of the area west of the Continental Divide. The exception is Vail and other ski areas that are considered to be in the mountains or **High Country**, even though they are on the Western Slope. The largest town on the Western Slope is Grand Junction, the hotbed of the newly retired. Unlike the St. Louis Arch, a gateway to the flat prairies of Kansas, Grand Junction is the staging area for many of the West's most beautiful natural monuments, beginning with the Colorado National Monument and ending at Arizona's Grand Canyon.

There is another divide that the weather people use, but don't explain and that is the **Palmer Divide**. It is a 7600 foot high ridge between Colorado Springs and Denver. Coming down its steep grade creates nasty winter driving conditions on I-25 near the Douglas County line or what is referred to as **Monument Hill.**

The term **Four Corners** refers to a piece of Indian land on the southwest corner of Colorado. It was added just for you tourists and is the only place in the country where you can see four different states at the same time: Arizona, Utah, New Mexico and Colorado. It is our one-ups-man-ship to Tennessee's Lookout Mountain, where you can see just three states. This Colorado out-cropping is one thing that keeps our state from being a perfect rectangle, in spite of how it appears on a map.

Colorado is the eighth largest state (387 miles by 276 miles), although if truth be told and you flattened all those hills and mountains, we'd actually be larger than Texas! People are bound to get lost. If you lose your way while hiking, just look for pyramid-shaped rock piles called cairns. They were left to help guide you and mark the trail. Along the Front Range use the mountains as giant westward cairns and pray it's not one of those rare cloudy days.

Where in Denver?

Any Colorado map will indicate the two interstates that intersect Colorado at Denver. Here's a few things that the maps don't tell you about navigating our largest city.

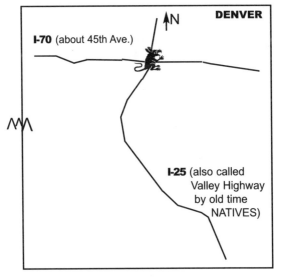

If you are at the intersection of these two interstates, you are caught in the **Mousetrap**. It's not only that you can't move anywhere, it's that the cars appear to multiply exponentially. At least you'll find the landscaping is nice.

Overall Denver has an easy grid system with the mountains to the west. You should note that Ellsworth Avenue runs east and west and is the dividing line for north and south avenues. Broadway runs north and south and is the east/west dividing line for the streets that parallel it.

Avenues north of Ellsworth
are numbered 1 to 160th. The ones
you need to know to get around
town are shown on the following
map. Colfax Avenue, which takes
the place of 15th Avenue, is the
longest continuous street in the
country (forty miles) and rightfully
deserves a name of its own.

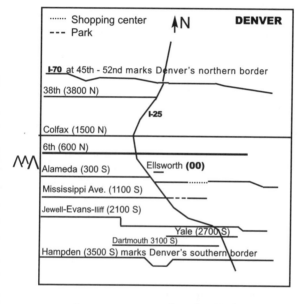

Avenues south of Ellsworth
are clustered in state names, college names and miscellaneous. The
east/west routes are often inter-
rupted by parks, malls, the interstate, railroads and poor long-term
planning. Sometimes you'll be zip-
ping along and the avenue takes a
jog and, before you know it, the
name changes. See Jewell-Evans-
Iliff. Try to remember the hundred
block associated with the avenue or
street and you should do fine.

Streets west of Broadway
parallel the mountains to the west.
The exception is Santa Fe Drive,
which is a diagonal discussed later.
Street names run in a single alphabet from Acoma to Zuni and desig-
nate American Indian tribes. The
single alphabet repeats after Zuni,
using surnames out to the suburbs.

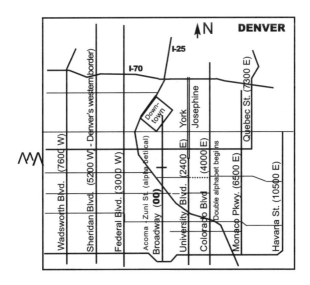

Streets east of Broadway
should be memorized to Colorado
Boulevard (forty blocks), since there
is no pattern. It's handy to know
that University becomes two one-
way streets–York and Josephine
north of 1st Avenue. East of
Colorado Boulevard names start
with double alphabets, the second
usually a flower, tree or bush
(Albion 4100E and Ash 4200E).
This pattern, minus the plant reference, repeats itself ad nauseam,
that is, eastward into the suburbs.

So, if you're driving along and notice two street names beginning with the same letter, chances are you are east of Colorado Boulevard. If you see street names in a single alphabet, then chances are you are west of Broadway. And if you're caught asking directions, we'll just figure you're a non-NATIVE.

By now you've caught on that many of the major north/south streets do not follow the naming pattern and are often called boulevards, parkways or drives. These are the ones that are referred to the most, especially during morning traffic reports. See maps. They are also the main exit designations for major thoroughfares through town.

Diagonals serve two purposes, shortcuts and confusion for the directionally challenged. They often have name changes which increase the fun. Speer Boulevard jogs south to Cherry Creek Drive (CCD on map), then jogs north to Leetsdale Drive and finally becomes Parker Road in the suburbs. Santa Fe Drive is continuous and multi-laned. Thus it encourages speeding and attracts the police, who must meet monthly quotas. Then there is the cluster of diagonal one-way streets we call downtown.

The **downtown** area is angled differently from Denver's grid system.

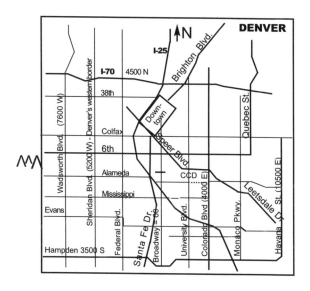

There are many stories about why this occurred. One is that downtown was laid out along Cherry Creek, while the rest of Denver was laid out along the Platte River. Another is that there were two separate towns that joined as populations increased.

Both are partially correct. Henry C. Brown of Brown Palace fame bought land east of downtown. He decided to follow the true compass directions for this Capitol Hill area instead of copying downtown's angled streets. One last theory involves an alcoholic architect. Feel free to make up your own urban legend and realize there are no rules for driving downtown. Just get used to going in circles, like a true NATIVE, when negotiating all those alternating one-way streets.

Other areas you need to know when talking about downtown,

include Auraria and LoDo. **Auraria** (Latin for gold) lies near lower downtown Denver and has its own exit from I-25, a kind of backdoor to the skyscrapers. Auraria refers to our state's largest college complex–the combined campuses of Metro State College, University of Colorado at Denver and the Community College of Denver.

   LoDo or lower downtown is adjacent to and part of downtown. It is more known for cafes, residential lofts and entertainment than office buildings. It is made up of three-to-four story, older brick buildings that were once used as warehouses and brothels. It still attracts young, single people who are looking for a good time.

DOWNTOWN DIVERSIONS

Take a friend and have formal tea at the Brown Palace.

Take an informal walking tour of LoDo by contacting the Colorado Historical Society for specifics.

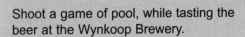

Ride the 16th Street shuttle until you find a restaurant, a shop or somebody you'd like to explore more fully.

Shoot a game of pool, while tasting the beer at the Wynkoop Brewery.

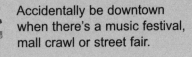

Accidentally be downtown when there's a music festival, mall crawl or street fair.

Where in Tarnation?

A mountain pass or ski resort is not necessarily near the town of the same name! This is included to save you from committing a non-NATIVE and down right embarrassing blunder.

When a friend came from Illinois to ski at Loveland, yours truly got out a map and headed for the city of Loveland, north of Denver. Although famous for canceling tons of mail on Valentine's Day, the town of Loveland is nowhere near the ski resort of the same name. To ski Loveland go west on I-70 from Denver and exit just before the Eisenhower Tunnel.

There is also a town called Berthoud, north of Denver, that has nothing to do with the on-again, off-again Berthoud ski area and Berthoud Pass, both in the mountains near Winter Park.

And although Keystone is a ski resort (and a beer), it is not the name of a town in Colorado. Dillon is where you go to ski at Keystone Resort.

As if that isn't enough, in Colorado five passes hold the title of Ute Pass and over forty streams claim the name Coal Creek.

Grand Junction actually refers to the junction of the Gunnison River and the Grand River now called the Colorado River. That is how Grand Valley and Grand Lake, originally referring to the river, got their names.

And Lookout Mountain is not a warning, but rather the final resting place of Buffalo Bill Cody. It is west of Denver near Golden and is a good spot for watching Fourth of July fireworks with the NATIVES, who don't know any better. There's no sense telling you the good spots or they wouldn't be good any more.

San Luis, southwest of Pueblo, is not a NATIVE way to say St. Louis. Rather it is the oldest community still in existence in Colorado. It was built in 1851, quite new by Boston standards.

And don't look for Boulder Dam (aka Hoover Dam) near the town of Boulder, Colorado. Boulder Dam is in Nevada. The Boulder Turnpike or US 36, however, does go to Boulder and is the infamous home of the University of Colorado. Even though it is still called a turnpike, it is no longer a toll road and you don't have to pay to use it.

Often you'll hear a weatherperson refer to a particular county. There are sixty-four in the state, about fifteen of which have fewer than 5000 people. I doubt even a NATIVE can tell you where most of the counties are, unless they happen to live there. The newest one, created in 2001, is Broomfield north of Denver. Denver is both a city and a county, having the largest population and the smallest land mass.

For those baffled by all the "Rocky" nomenclature, a flagrant fixation forced onto federal facilities, here is some clarification. Glowin' in the wind **Rocky Flats** northwest of Denver once made triggers and other parts for plutonium weapons and is known for having the largest industrial fire in the country back in 1969. The **Rocky Mountain Arsenal** northeast of Denver is now a not-so-toxic bird and wildlife sanctuary. In 1965 pressurized well waste dumpings there caused 700 earth tremors before someone realized the relationship and closed the wells. You won't glow in the dark if you eat our famous melons from **Rocky Ford** (not Flats), a farming area along the Arkansas Valley in southeastern Colorado.

If you're confused and female ask directions. If you're a guy, you're never confused and wouldn't a GPS be more fun? If you are not sure if you are male or female, check out Trinidad. Although it prefers to be recognized as the rugged roost of 1882 Marshall Bat Masterson, it is considered the sex-change capital of the world. When we say Colorful Colorado, we're not just talkin' scenery.

DIVERSIONS FOR RAIL FANS

For some the only way to travel is on one of the three foot wide narrow gauge railroads, such as the **Durango and Silverton** in the state's southwest corner or the **Cumbres and Toltec** on the New Mexico border. The **Georgetown Loop** (46 miles west of Denver) crosses itself to gain altitude. Standard gauge fare (4 ft. 8.5 in. wide) includes Denver's **Winter Park Ski Train, Amtrak**'s scenic equivalent, which continues past Grand Junction and the **Royal Gorge Route** in Cañon City.

For little rail fans, there are some inexpensive train experiences, open only in the summer. One loops around the lake at **Lakeside Amusement Park** (4601 Sheridan Blvd. in Denver) and the second circles around **Tiny Town** (southwest of Denver at 6249 S. Turkey Creek Road). The last two are in Metro Denver at **Belleview Park** and **Hudson Gardens**. For bigger kids there is the **Colorado Railroad Museum** (exit 265 off I-70 at 17155 W. 44th Ave. in Golden) or the **Forney Transportation Museum** (4303 Brighton Blvd. in Denver), which includes other modes or as they put it–Anything on Wheels!

Other mobile interests include the **Stanley Steamer Museum** (333 E. Wonderview Ave. in Estes Park), where you can tour the Stanley Hotel and meet some ghosts, the **Mountain Biking Hall of Fame** (200 Sopris Street in Crested Butte), which includes a heritage museum of the town, and a boat ride alongside the Arkansas River at the **Riverwalk in Pueblo**.

NATIVE Drivers

If you're driving to Colorado from the West, you can't beat the scenery. If you're arriving via the East, be prepared for miles and miles of monotony. Missouri boasts its biggest attractions as fireworks and adult stores, if you go by the billboards scattered along I-70. The Show Me state's nickname suggests that we take them literally.

Midwesterners will notice less water and fewer bridges on the way here. Trees shrink in size and quantity. Dry, intense sunlight replaces humidity as you rise in altitude. The haze lifts and the gray sky turns bluer with each passing mile. But then eastern Colorado appears and it looks just like Kansas! How can that be? Keep searching the horizon. On a clear day you can see Pike's Peak, just as Zebulon Pike did, about eighty miles east of Denver. Before you know it you're in the city and part of our traffic congestion. Now that you have chosen Colorado as your new home, here are a few survivor driving tips.

In Colorado there is a saying, "the shortest distance between two points is a construction project." So, when you see a "Give 'em a brake!" sign near these project sites, it really means slam on your brakes.

Construction folks, like many drivers here, rarely give you enough warning to figure out what they are up to.

Remember the old car commercial "Stay between the lines, the lines are our friends"? Well, they aren't in Colorado. Lines are like fences and we don't want to be fenced in. So when you notice every other driver straddling the lane lines, they aren't necessarily drunk, asleep or on a cell phone, although that may be the case. Generally Coloradans are road hogs and as difficult as it seems, just get used to it and "Be careful out there."

Going for a drive? There's nothing like spending a fun-filled, relaxing weekend among the breathtakingly serene mountains to forget about work. Unfortunately all that sense of well-being is lost during the tension-filled, Indy-like I-70 race back to Denver. Throw in some snow and a few trucks without chains and your peaceful weekend turns into a white-knuckled blur.

Remember the old college ruse: How many people can you fit into a Volkswagen Beetle? Denver's grown-up version is–how many cars can

I BRAKE FOR RACKS

If there seems to be a lot of police cars in your rear view mirror, look again. Those are ski and bike racks, not flashing lights, on top of all those vehicles.

you get through an intersection after the light has turned red? Never, ever anticipate the green light in Denver. Your life may depend upon it.

Another favorite pastime is bumper cars. Unlike Florida with its alligators, we have an even more dangerous predator called the tail-gator. It's amazing, but Colorado drivers now care more about saving a few minutes over saving a few lives–possibly even their own. This is a clear cut case of non-NATIVISM.

Two other kinds of drivers to watch out for are:

• **Creeps**-These are the folks, who are so impatient to merge or turn into your lane, that they creep toward you before you've driven past them. Your reaction is to slow down and thus, get hit by them, or swerve out of their way and hit someone else.

• **Rouletters**-These are the people who can't wait to see around the curve or over the next hill before passing you. They like to play Russian roulette with their cars. Can they pass you before hitting the oncoming car or will the oncoming car slow down to avoid a collision?

Got turn signals? Most cars in Colorado seem to be defective.

Public transportation is still a new concept here. Recent trends show Colorado's vehicles now out-number actual Coloradans. In fact we've outnumbered the available parking spots for years. Keep a lot of quarters handy. Even in neighborhoods everyone parks on the street, since our garages are full of sports equipment and other stuff. We spend so much time in our cars, we actually measure distance by time. Thus, you should say, "It is 30 **minutes** to ___" not "20 **miles** to___." Coloradans treat their cars like American Express®, they never leave home without them.

Are there fewer and fewer NATIVES on the road? Are the drivers denser than the traffic? When did road rage become all the rage? All I know is, Coloradans are as friendly as they ever were, unless you meet them behind a steering wheel.

TROLLEYS REINCARNATED

In the 1880s Denver installed a cable car system that was quickly replaced by the electric trolley. They stayed in service until 1950. Ninety percent of Denverites depended on them prior to WWII, when cars took over. Now Denver has brought them back at a much higher cost and with a new name–Light Rail. As of 2004 these electric lines run from Broadway and Alameda to LoDo and follow Santa Fe Drive south to Mineral. By 2007 there will be service to the Denver Tech Center, paralleling I-25. More routes are planned.

How Many Are There?

"I thought Denver had more than 5280 people." That number under the city name is the elevation, silly, not the population. Since signs note only the altitude, be prepared to be as ignorant as the rest of us on the actual population of various cities. Statewide we are 4.4 million strong and growing.

If you must show off, a good estimate for Denver city and county is half a million. For the Greater Metro Area we're approaching two million. No longer a cow town, we are large enough to have every possible fast food chain and retail outlet known to America.

Not to confuse you, but street signs are in white letters with a green background and license plates are in green letters with a white background (except for the recent trend to vary the color on personalized plates). You'd think since Colorado means "red" in Spanish that the signs or plates would be in red, but I digress.

To win a NATIVE's heart, feel free to show off your knowledge of the following city populations from the 2000 census. These populations, gathered from the 2003 World Almanac, are for towns greater than 5000.

Colorado's Largest Communities

(Numbers are in the 1000's for the year 2000.)

Pop.	Denver Metro
555	Denver
276	Aurora
144	Lakewood
103	Centennial*
102	Arvada
101	Westminster
82	Thornton
71	Highlands Ranch
44	Southglenn
40	Littleton
38	Broomfield
33	Wheat Ridge
32	Englewood
32	Northglenn
31	Ken Caryl
24	Parker
21	Commerce City
21	Brighton

80% of Coloradans live along the Front Range. Favorite place names include Damifino Park and the towns of Crook and Beshoar Junction.

Pop.	Foothills
17	Golden
9	Evergreen

Most resort towns are small, which is hard to believe when you are jammed into a T-shirt shop with a few hundred tourists.

Pop.	Front Range
361	Colorado Sprgs
119	Fort Collins
103	Pueblo
95	Boulder
77	Greeley
71	Longmont
51	Loveland
23	Lafayette
20	Castle Rock
16	Cañon City

Pop.	Western Slope
42	Grand Junction
14	Durango
12	Montrose

Pop.	Ski/Resorts
10	Steamboat Sprgs
8	Glenwood Sprgs
6	Aspen

*This 2001 figure is a new town formed from unincorporated areas.

Mavericks Wanted

If you came here to launch a new business, you are in the right place. Name your business Rocky Mountain this or Mile High that, if you want to be truly NATIVE. And don't forget to use a mountain logo for the company stationery.

Small businesses with less than twenty employees make up about 86% of Colorado's companies. We rank in the top four in educational degrees per capita, but also have one of the worst high school graduation rates in the US. And we are workaholics, often falling asleep while driving or conducting business on a cell phone.

JOB HUNTING

Start your job search at the Denver Public Library at 10 West Fourteenth Avenue. It is considered one of the best in the nation, when it's not closed due to budget cuts. With branch libraries, you can check out books on line, have them delivered to the branch closest to your home and avoid driving downtown.

Unions here are rare unless you work for the government, do construction or teach in the public schools. This is because of the current emphasis on small businesses and the historic emphasis on distribution. In the 1980's this non-union atmosphere created the perception and the realty that you had to sacrifice pay to live here. Today our state's salaries match the national average. Unfortunately it seems as if the cost of living exceeds that national average, which may explain our workaholic attitude.

Major businesses include tourism, agriculture (most income from livestock), service industries, high tech and academic research, construction, health care, finance and insurance. There are also 16,000 non-profit organizations here and that doesn't even include the ones that are poorly managed.

There are two major employment clusters in the Denver Metro area. DTC or the Denver Tech Center includes the Inverness area and is southeast of the city along I-25. The more obvious place to work is in downtown Denver, where all the tall buildings are located.

MAVERICK PERSONIFIED

KBPI radio manager Bill Pierson refused to vacate the D & F Tower when this Denver landmark closed to the public in 1965. When the city turned off the utilities, he stopped paying his lease. He did negotiate electricity to broadcast, but had no elevator or water. He and his employees climbed 469 stairs and brought in their food and water until the lease ran out about two years later.

In spite of recent scandals to the contrary, women are and have been treated fairly in Colorado. In fact women are one of the best-represented groups in the state. Just in case you don't believe me, as of July 2003 Colorado tied Maryland with the highest percentage of women state representatives (33%), second only to Washington state.

Women-owned businesses are one reason small firms succeed in Colorado. After all, one way to get rid of that glass ceiling is to build your own house! Women here got the vote in 1893, twenty-seven years before the US passed the 19th amendment.

Whereas Texans claim Ike Eisenhower, we claim his wife Mamie, who grew up in Denver. And back when lawyers conjured up respect, instead of jokes, the American Bar Association admitted its first woman lawyer in 1917–Mary Lathrop, a Denverite. NATIVES also claim the name for the Tony Awards from Antoinette Perry, who got her theatrical start at old Elitch Gardens. Frances Jacobs sparked the charity movement that resulted in the United Way. Florence Sabin, the first female full professor at John Hopkins Medical School, made all our lives healthier. She retired in Denver in 1946, helped reduce the state's infant mortality by half and helped pass laws to improve sanitary conditions.

If you speak both English and Spanish, you'll be more marketable here. There are thousands of Hispanic-owned companies. Making up about 28% of Denver's and 17% of Colorado's population, you can't get much more NATIVE, unless you are Native American.

THE TAXING SITUATION

Colorado ranks 22nd of 50 states in its combined tax burden with one being the highest. The state tax is relatively low compared to other states (45th), but when combined with all the local taxes (7th), it brings it toward the middle.

State income tax rate   4.63%
(as percent of federal taxable income)

Retail Sales   7.2%
(varies based on city and county)

State	2.9%
County	1.0%
City	2.5%
RTD	0.8%

Residential Property Tax   10-15%
(as percent of assessed value)

State Gas Tax   22%

Vehicle Licensing & Property Tax
(declines by age of vehicle, based on taxable value, meaning the original sticker price)

Year	Rate
1	2.1%
2	1.5%
3	1.2%
4	0.9%
5	.45%

*All information is for the year 2001.

History of Employment

In spite of its gold rush beginnings and the importance of mining throughout Colorado, the state rarely sustained a large number of unskilled laborers. The lack of water discouraged manufacturers and distribution became key. Many entrepreneurs earned their fortunes investing in and later supplying miners, ranchers and farmers with the gear necessary to do their work. If you live along the Front Range long enough, you will recognize the names of many of these early entrepreneurs: Brown, Boettcher, May, Cheesman, Tabor, Phipps, Daniels, Penrose, Elitch, Byers, Palmer, Bonfils, Evans, Coors and Gates.

Land was first irrigated and farmed for food to support workers. After railroads supplied these crops, farmers grew grains to feed the more profitable, four-legged livestock. The barbed wire put farming back in vogue, despite setbacks from grasshoppers, drought and blizzards. Today's non-livestock products are flowers and greenhouse plants, grains, fruit, especially melons and grapes for wine, potatoes and sugar beets. Plants account for 31% of agricultural income. Less than 1% of workers are now involved in mining, yet it remains one of the highest paying industries.

MY WIRED VALENTINE

John Valentine came to Denver as a
lawyer. He invested in a floral company
with nurseries at East High School, stud-
ied flowers and in 1910 started the
Florists' Telegraph (now Transworld)
Delivery Association or FTD, a coopera-
tive owned by member florists. Valentine
died in a car accident at 58. Annual
sales are now over $500 million.

If you study Colorado's history,
you'll see a recurring theme. Much
like a bronco buster, the state gets
thrown by economic downturns,
but quickly dusts itself off and gets
right back into the
entrepreneurial saddle.
Wages here seem to be
related to which side of
the boom/bust tight-
rope you happen to be on. You
could be rolling in money one year
and waiting tables the next.

Exxon kick-started one boom
in the 1970s near Grand Junction.
Oil prices were soaring, and they
had the five billion dollar idea of
extracting oil from shale. Colorado
has enough shale oil to power the
entire country. Although drillers
Marvin Davis and Phillip Anschutz
became billionaires during this
time, the economy was busted by
1982. Oil prices dipped and Exxon
abandoned their plans. Their with-
drawal on May 2 is still known as
Black Sunday. It's reassuring to
know that if gas prices ever get high

enough to make shale oil extraction profitable, Colorado will again be sitting on a gold mine, so to speak.

The 2001 bust in the high tech industry and the reversal of fortunes tied to large employers means there are quite a few baby boomers, who'll be working much longer to reach that permanent siesta time known as retirement.

ENTREPRENEURIAL CUISINE

One infamous businessman guided a group from Utah to the southern Colorado gold mines and got lost. Alferd (not Alfred) Packer survived the winter of 1873-74 by eating all his customers! He is buried in Littleton, a suburb of Denver.

Although small businesses bring volatility and are more susceptible to economic ups and downs, they also bring innovations. You can thank entrepreneurial Coloradans for:

- The ice cream soda
- The cheeseburger
- Shredded wheat
- FTD-wiring flowers nationwide
- Aluminum beer cans
- Steel studded tires
- The United Way
- The Waterpik®
- Softball
- The Denver boot
- Diagonal crosswalk signals

Where to Live

Most people who move to Colorado end up living where there are the most jobs, that is, on the Eastern Slope between Fort Collins and Pueblo. Most often this means Denver.

Years ago when Jesse Jackson came to Denver's African-American neighborhood at Five Points, he supposedly quipped, "You call this a ghetto? Where I come from this is considered middle class." There are no bad neighborhoods in Colorado cities, especially when compared to the likes of Chicago's infamous Cabrini Green. The most dangerous place to live seems to be the Air Force Academy in Colorado Springs, especially for female cadets.

Families flock to the suburbs so they can be close to the larger malls and each other. Single folks or childless couples think Denver is a great place to live.

The Capitol Hill neighborhood near the state capitol attracts non-NATIVE newbies and renters, when they first arrive in Denver. They like the area for its accessibility to downtown jobs, brewpubs and nightlife, not necessarily in that order. These renters seem to have fewer rights than home owners. In Illinois, landlords had to pay interest on damage deposits. Here you're lucky to get your deposits back in full, regardless of how conscientious you are to the premises.

Many of the beautiful turn-of-the-century buildings are apartment houses, once called terraces. Do not be insulted if someone says, "Look, a **Denver square**." They are not talking about you, but rather a box-like, two-to-three-story home with a porch, built sometime between 1900 and WWI. Another style you should know is the **bungalow**–a one to one-and-a-half story home popular between 1920 and 1940, known for its open spaces and built-in cabinets. Denver has preserved many of its older homes, often made of brick. As in Chicago, fires made brick the preferred building material in Denver. Painted brick is common and helps preserve the aging mortar. Now that you're out of the Midwest, fit in by painting your house anything but white.

Acquaint yourself with these new construction terms. They became popular when commuters decided to move back to the city and renovate older homes. A **pop-top** refers to removing the roof of a single story building and adding a second or third floor, virtually eliminating sun exposure to adjacent homes. A **scrape**, on the other hand, means that a home is completely torn down and replaced with a sprawling suburban eyesore that leaves little green space and stands out like a sore thumb in a neighborhood of quaint homes and tree-lined streets. Whew! New legislation requiring more green space and new neighborhood associations guiding developers are addressing these concerns.

With the clean up of Denver's railroad yards, there are many newly-built places to live in close to downtown. For home buyers there are also new housing developments at the old Stapleton Airport and the former Lowry Air Force Base. Be one of the first to own a place at the redevelopment of the Gates complex on either side of Broadway just south of I-25.

Ski bums and nature lovers quickly find out how expensive it is to live in the mountains near resort communities. If you get off the well-beaten tourist paths, you'll see areas in resort towns filled with trailer courts. These are referred to by NATIVES as "slave quarters," where hard-working, minimum wage workers live.

Housing costs are frustrating no matter where you are. In my neighborhood most folks could not afford to buy their homes today. But in 1989 they were priced at one fourth what they are now. The worst part is that as a workaholic who spends weekends in the mountains, you'll have little time to appreciate any part of your new home–except, perhaps, the bed-room!

Risky Business

Whether you participate in the office sports pool, play lotto or enjoy slot machines, gambling is alive and controlled in Colorado.

We all felt sympathetic when Black Hawk, Cripple Creek and Central City pleaded for gambling to salvage their dying small town economies. Newcomers only see what the towns are now. NATIVES remember their quaintness before they were scraped of their character and left looking like open wounds. Which is why we haven't expanded gambling to other towns, nor voted for an increase in the bets now limited to five dollars. Ironically, a portion of the gambling proceeds, that are taxed at 18%, go to historic preservation. In fact, Colorado is second only to Florida in its preservation spending.

State lottery or Lotto proceeds go to parks, recreation and open spaces after the winners are paid. Coloradans may also play Powerball.

YEAH, I'LL BET!

The last major Indian attack in Colorado happened in 1870 when Ute Indian Agent Nathan Meeker plowed up their horse race track to stop their gambling. He and 14 others were killed. The Utes were moved to reservations and ironically had the last say. They now operate one casino in Ignacio and one in Towaoc.

Ethnicity

Colorado is a mixed bag in more ways than one. Where else does a Hispanic mayor step down to work for the President of the United States and have two African-American successors vie for his job? It makes me proud.

But don't get the wrong idea, bigotry has a long tradition in Colorado. Past political leaders were Ku Klux Klan members during the hate revival of the 1920s. The old airport was named after a sympathizer–Benjamin Stapleton. The media still make a bigger deal about Hispanic joy riders during Cinco de Mayo, than they do "excitable" white Bronco football fans vandalizing downtown after a Super Bowl victory.

KARMA FOR IDIOTS

The Ku Klux Klan was disbanded in 1871, revived after WWI and reached its peak in 1924. "Recruiters" worked like a pyramid scheme, getting 40% of the initiation fee. Originally targeting blacks, Catholics and Jews, their hatred later included liberals, union members and the foreign born. They burned crosses at the top of Ruby Hill in Denver and at Castle Rock on south Table Mountain above Coors Brewery in Golden. They controlled the governor, mayor of Denver, Secretary of State, and several judges, but lost favor by enforcing Prohibition too strongly. The ex-governor later served 5 years for mail fraud.

Instinctively I feel less antebellum "baggage" here in the West. The Civil War wounds do not run as deeply as back East. I do not get as many stares if I am with a person of color, but I have been stopped by the police for riding in a car with one.

GLORIETTA PASS

There were about 5000 Coloradans who served in the Civil War. In 1862 Union troops with Colorado volunteers kept Confederates from capturing the gold at Pike's Peak and Denver. The skirmish was called the Gettysburg of the West. Its leader John Chivington later killed innocent Indian women and children at Sand Creek.

If color isn't enough, we also have a large gay and lesbian community that helps take the pressure off the other minorities from time to time. Guess that's how Denver got the nickname "Queen City of the Plains."

Not only are some NATIVES homophobic, they are also "lingo-phobic." The joke now is that with so many Spanish speakers willing to take back-breaking, low-paying jobs, employers are forced to learn

THE GAY '60s

Evenings at the state capitol were dominated by male hookers in the 1960s. The road around it was known as "the fruit loop."

their employee's language just to communicate with them.

How soon we forget! Between Coronado's gold rush in 1540 to the Dominguez-Escalante 2000 mile trek in 1776 (before Lewis and Clark's big adventure), the Spanish had settled southern Colorado for over 200 years. They ventured here to mine, to go after marauding Indians and to discourage the French from creeping into their territory. But Manifest Destiny prevailed and the US won the area by war with Mexico in 1848.

> It is said that Mexicans didn't cross the border, but rather the border crossed them.

Many of the terms related to mining and herding come from these settlers, including bonanza, cinch, mesa, chaps, rodeo, stampede, lariat, buckaroo, ranch and burro. Perhaps we should be teaching Spanish to all our children at an early age, when it is so much simpler to learn. America has no official language, but over half the states, including Colorado, have passed laws making English their *official* language. Up until 1900 the official languages of Colorado were English, German and Spanish.

LOST IN TRANSLATION

Coors Brewery once had the slogan "Turn it Loose," which in Spanish translated as "Suffer from Diarrhea."

Colorado parallels America in its ethnic population. The largest, non-

Hispanic, immigrant groups arriving after 1876 came from Germany, Great Britain and Italy.

Germans were the most successful, especially in the business of brewing. Their rise resulted in an 1877 law requiring German to be taught in public schools. Their fall came with Prohibition and WWI, when speaking German was forbidden in all schools.

Many Colorado Irish were already assimilated, having come from Canada or the East. Mostly Catholic they came with their growing families and worked in mining and railroading, as well as in saloons and law enforcement. When Pope John Paul II made an appearance in Colorado in August 1993, it was the largest gathering in our history–400,000. Denver's first St. Patrick Day parade was 100 years earlier. It disappeared after WWI and came back with gusto in the 1960s and today is one of the largest in the US.

The British influence came in the form of money and land sales. The lack of land in England had wealthy fathers buying huge parcels in the West for their children's inheritance. This was how William Jackson Palmer built the Denver and Rio Grande Railroad and Little London, or what we call Colorado Springs today. The English invested in Colorado's mining, railroading and ranching industries and their influence still shows in Denver's architecture, namely the Oxford Hotel. In 1883 the British invested over half a million dollars in the seventy-four mile long Highline Canal. It was their contribution to suburban farming and put Littleton, a Denver suburb, on the map as an agricultural center. Like other irrigation ditches it is still in use today and now parallels a National Landmark Trail bikeway.

Italians farmed at the Denver railroad yards near the South Platte River. Their descendants still run wholesale produce companies there. Italians built the Manitou and Pikes Peak Cog Railway in 1889, which goes to the top of Pikes Peak. It was financed by Beautyrest® bed maker Zalmon Simmons, after he almost maimed himself riding to the summit on a burro. One famous Italian was Mother Cabrini, the first American saint, whose shrine is west of Denver at the Morrison exit. The Italian influence is celebrated on Columbus Day with two parades in Denver–one by the Italians and the other, an anti-Columbus parade, by the American Indians.

WHERE THERE'S A WILL . . .

Angelo Noce lobbied nationally for a Columbus Day holiday. He succeeded in Colorado in 1907. By 1922 when Noce died, 35 states had followed. It became a national holiday in 1968.

ETHNIC DIVERSIONS

The **Colorado Springs Fine Arts Center** built in 1936 at 30 West Dale Street features Hispanic and Native American art, as does the **Denver Art Museum** at 100 West 14th.

The Hue-man Experience at 911 Park Ave West in Denver is the largest US African-American bookstore. **The Black American West Museum** at 3091 California Street is an eye opener. Did you know that one in every three cowboys was black? Or that Abe Lincoln's one-time bodyguard was a black man, who came to Colorado and operated a barber shop and podiatry business?

Sakura Square at 1255 19th Street in Denver is a cultural center for Japanese. It honors Governor Ralph Carr for his fair treatment of the 7600 Japanese-Americans interned at the Amache Camp near Granada after Pearl Harbor. Carr was not re-elected and little remains of the camp.

The Denver Turnverein at 1570 Clarkson Street is Denver's oldest ethnic club. Purchased in 1922, Germans used it until it was open to all in the 1990s. A room full of German memorabilia is under development.

The Trinidad History Museum at 300 East Main offers an extensive view of Hispanic life and history and is well worth the time.

The **Folklorist Program** funded by the Colorado Council on the Arts at Greeley, Alamosa, Denver and Grand Junction includes oral histories, music, dance, craft and cooking displays of early settlers.

The Swedes and Chinese did not survive the racial attitudes of Colorado. Scandinavian bachelors did not marry and often went back East or to their native country. However, many Canadians and Minnesotans with Scandinavian names have migrated here. The most famous Denver Swede was Reverend Edgar Wahlberg, who helped to create jobs for the poor during the Depression and later on during the War on Poverty.

The Chinese were the only ethnic group excluded by law from immigrating to America. Their cheap labor was a threat, especially during the economic depression of the mid-1870s. Halloween 1880 marks their virtual disappearance from Denver, when a race riot burned Hop Alley, their business center near downtown. It is ironic that the Chinese, who were associated with opium dens, actually resisted importation of it to China, but the English insisted and won via the Opium Wars of the 1840s and 1850s.

In the last thirty years, Thai. Chinese, Vietnamese and other Southeast Asians have made themselves known and formed their own productive neighborhoods in the Denver Metro area. You'll come to know them for some of the best-tasting, reasonably-priced restaurants in town.

How to Dress—Clothing Optional

Fit in by wearing the right clothes or, if at a hot springs, no clothes at all.

If you want to see someone in a suit, check out downtown Denver. People-watching on the 16th Street Mall will orient you as to style or lack thereof. And it is a fun pastime. Otherwise jeans or khakis will suffice. You will not see as many bolo ties or turquoise jewelry as you might think. Boots and cowboy hats are not the fashion statement they once were–not in the city anyway. Nothing says tourist more than a gold-colored aspen leaf dangling from your ears. So give them away to one of your non-NATIVE relatives.

Learn to layer. For NATIVES layering means to wear several thin articles of clothing on top of one another, so you can strip one off as the sun pops out or put one back on if it dives behind the mountains.

LAYER LIST

Layering includes T-shirts, blouses, light sweaters, fleece, vests and windbreakers, long underwear for high country ice-skating and thin, wicking breathable fabrics for skiing. Moisture-proof boots (no leather soles or worn tennis shoes) are for hiking and sandals are for trekking out to the hot tub or hot springs. Don't forget the slippers for lounging in front of the fire.

58

Layering is also reassuring if you
don't know what to wear. One of
those combinations should work.

A NATIVE is always prepared.
Even summer nights can be quite
cool. Keep a windbreaker or
pullover close at hand–the fleecer
the better. As always, wear furs at
your own risk, but never in
Boulder. Boulderites look at fur
coats the way a spray-painting
teenager looks at a blank wall.

Remember that we are sports
enthusiasts here and by golly we're
proud to pay for all the special
clothes, goggles, helmets, gloves
and boots necessary for the full
outdoor experience. And that's just
for the spectators. Do not
be alarmed if you see someone dressed in tight-fitting
lycra shorts that look as if
he or she didn't quite make
it to the bathroom. Not to worry,
it's just a sporty fashion statement,
unless there isn't a bicycle close by.

"Mirror, mirror on the wall,
who's the most high tech clothing
wearer of all?"

CAN YOU AFFORD TO SKI?

	Equipment	Clothes
Rent	$15/day	n/a
Buy Used	$300	$100
Buy New	$500-700	$220-750

Find discount tickets if skiing for just a day.
Tickets at resorts are 30-50% more. A 3-
day pass averages $40-$50/day. Season
passes start at $200 with limitations and
climb from there.

Being a Sports Fan–NOT Optional!

Sports is to a NATIVE what the Lone Star is to a Texan. To give you a clearer idea, back in the late 1970s or early 1980s a gentleman in a bar began playing the jukebox during a Bronco game. An angry fan went home, got his gun, came back and killed the guy. The jury was more sympathetic to the some-what-justified fan than the uncouth victim and reduced the sentence from first to second degree murder.

I have to admit that even I watched the Broncos for years, but their constant choking and last minute Heimlich maneuvers wore me out. I know them's fightin' words. So, avoid the crowds, shop during a Bronco game and enjoy short lift lines by skiing on Super Bowl Sunday.

BRONCO BUST

Lawrence Phipps financially helped keep the Broncos in Denver despite their first eleven years without a winning season.

As a NATIVE you should know that the Elway Legacy actually refers to John's past quarterback-ing skills, not the Suburus that he sells. These days the closest I come to being a Bronco fan is to buy Eddie McAffrey's Rocky Mountain (what else?) Mustard.

In addition to football, Coloradans boast the Avalanche

(hockey), the Rockies (baseball) and the Rapids (soccer). Over the years the loyalty to the Nuggets (basketball) has been tied to their skill level, which seems to bounce up and down as often as the balls they dribble.

"PUCK"ER UP

Denver's Mammoth Gardens, now the Fillmore Auditorium, was home to the first professional hockey team called the Denver Americans. They only lasted a couple seasons in the mid-1930s.

Even back in 1983 you could root for five to seven key basketball players. Now they change teams faster than you can delete spam from your e-mail and brag about their tattoos instead of their field goals. Without the finesse of Alex English, the heart and great laugh of Bill Russell and, most important-ly, the short shorts of yesteryear, what's to watch? Today's game plan seems to be to hire players with prison records rather than scoring records. But I digress.

For me winter sports is ice skating outdoors on the five-acre frozen lake at Keystone Resort. You can skate to the tunes and thaw out near the bonfire with a cup of hot choco-late. Summer fun means squeezing the life out of my brakes, while

ACADEMICS WON, FOOTBALL 0

The University of Denver's only football loss in 1908 came from Jim Thorpe's Carlisle Indians. DU dropped football in 1961.

screaming down the mountain at thirty miles per hour. It is my reward for bicycling all the way to the top.

There are many individual sports activities in Colorado–from fishing to hunting, kayaking to rafting, hiking to climbing, mountain biking to urban "scootering." Now if they would just invent silencers to use on jet skies, snowmobiles, ATVs and dirt bikes, we could all enjoy nature's peace and quiet. Regardless of whether you like watching or participating in sports, you can still pass as a NATIVE by using sports metaphors to describe anything you do.

SMALL TOWN VICTORIES

In 1929 a little town named Joes made basketball history. So did its coach, Lane Sullivan, who'd never played the game. Joes, Colorado had a high school team made up of farm boys and no indoor gym. They won the state championship and placed third at the nationals in Chicago. The Windsor Wizards did it in 1924–the first team in the West to win the title. The Branson High School team revived the title, winning the 1967 Class A state finals.

Quiz Time

How many NATIVES know the state tree, flower, bird, animal, nickname, motto or song? Shame on you. Try to redeem yourself by answering the following:

1. The official state tree is:
   a) The Sequoia
   b) The Palm Tree
   c) The Tree your father said money didn't grow on
   d) The Colorado blue spruce

2. The official state flower is:
   a) The white & lavender columbine
   b) The sunflower
   c) The tumbling tumbleweed
   d) The willows

3. The official state bird is:
   a) The flamingo (only in Denver)
   b) The bird often flown by commuters during rush hour
   c) The bird of paradise
   d) The lark bunting or white-winged blackbird

4. The official state animal is:
   a) The prairie dog
   b) The golden retriever
   c) The Rocky Mountain bighorn sheep
   d) The Colorado Buffaloes

5. Colorado's nickname is:
   a) The Silver State
   b) The Centennial State
   c) The State of Confusion
   d) a and b (+c if you are confused.)

6. Colorado's official motto is:
   a) Nothing without money
   b) Nothing without a gold mine
   c) Nothing without the Rocky
      Mountains
   d) Nothing without Providence

7. The official state song is:
   a) Where the Columbines Grow
   b) Where the Buffaloes Roam
   c) Where the Boys Are
   d) Where There's Smoke There's
      Fire

Bonus Question:

8. The official state gemstone is:
   a) Fossil Stone
   b) Green Adventurine
   c) Aspen-shaped gold leaf
   d) Aquamarine

Answers are on the back of the last page.

DIVERSIONS

Bored? You shouldn't be. Do what
everyone who comes here does,
shop at Denver's Cherry
Creek Mall or check out our:

- 4 national parks
- 5 national monuments
- 40 state parks
- 12 wildlife and recreational areas
- 10 national forests
- 2 national grasslands
- 500+ fishable lakes

Colorado Centerfold

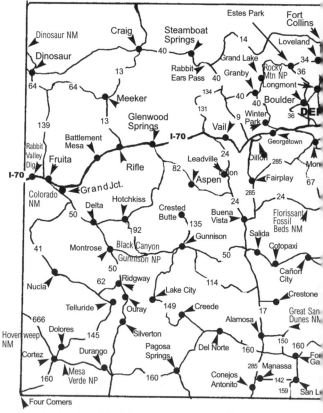

1" = 67 Miles = about 1 hr, 10 min

NP=National Park
NM=National Monument

MILES/TIME FROM DENVER

Aspen	157	3 3/4 hr
Black Canyon of Gunnison NP	262	5 1/4 hr
Burlington	170	2 3/4 hr
Colorado NM	263	4 3/4 hr
Colorado Springs	67	1+ hr
Dinosaur NM	333	7 1/2 hr
Durango	333	7 hr
Estes Park	72	1 1/2 hr
Florissant Fossil Beds NM	100	2 hr
Fort Collins	67	1+ hr
Glenwood Springs	157	2 1/2 hr
Grand Junction	243	4 hr
Greeley	66	1+ hr
Hovenweep NM	460	8 1/2 hr

Our obsession with time may be tied to the atomic clock in Boulder, the most accurate time piece in the world.

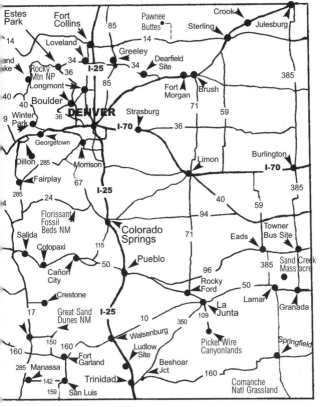

MILES/TIME FROM DENVER

Julesburg	186	3 hr
La Junta	172	3 hr
Lake City	251	5 1/3 hr
Mesa Verde NP	388	8 3/4 hr
Ouray	334	6 hr
Pagosa Springs	273	5 3/4 hr
Picket Wire Canyonlands	192	3 1/2 hr
Pueblo	110	1 3/4 hr
Rocky Mountain NP	88	2 1/3 hr
Sand Dunes NM/NP	237	4 1/2 hr
San Luis	222	4 hr
Springfield	275	5 1/4 hr
Steamboat Springs	156	3 1/3 hr
Telluride	364	6 3/4 hr
Trinidad	195	3 hr
Vail	97	1 3/4 hr

Weather or Not

Our biggest success at population control is that people think it snows as much along the Front Range urban areas as it does in the mountains. An occasional Monday night football game during a rare Denver blizzard helps keep that myth alive. Denver has been known to get dumped on. But that only happens when the weather person says the words "a few inches" and "upslope conditions" in the same sentence.

After a Denver blizzard, you'll find it is difficult to get around. Clean-up efforts seem to be in direct proportion to the current mayor's desire to be re-elected. Snow, because of the dry air, often melts before the city can get plows to your neighborhood. In fact here they plow snow back onto the streets after a storm for faster meltdown! Sometimes when Denver gets hit with snow, the mountains are clear and sunny.

Although the cities are fairly weather safe, when traveling in the mountains it is suggested that you keep a candle, granola bars, water, blanket, tire chains and for those caught in a very tight spot–the all important amputee kit. To give you an idea of the amount of snow possible, mountain towns used to have two-story outhouses!

BETWEEN A ROCK & A HARD PLACE

Even experienced climbers like Aron Ralston get in tight situations. In May 2003 pinned for five days by an 800-pound boulder and with no supplies left but a knife, he amputated his right arm. He was not the first to do this.

Road crews still sand roads around here. Unlike salt, which rusts your vehicle, the only bad thing about sand is the occasional rock that gets mixed in. Because of these, get used to cracked windshields, which are not always covered by your car insurance. With the current trend of using a liquid deicer, rusting problems are likely to make a comeback.

Chinook season is not when recreational vehicles hit the road, but rather a warm wind offering Front Range folks a winter reprieve. Literally, the Indian translation is "snow eater," and indeed these breezes do warm the snow enough to melt it. They usually arrive in January in time for Denver's National Western Stock Show and can make the air fragrant with *eau de bovine*. They have been known to raise temperatures by as much as twenty degrees.

You will look like a conspicuous non-NATIVE on a cloudy day if you walk around with an umbrella. With all the lightning strikes we get, you are more of a target carrying one anyway. Around here the only umbrellas you are likely to see are shading outdoor tables at the local coffeehouse or cafe.

Not to worry, those distant clouds often produce rain that never even hits the ground. This phenomenon is known as verga.

DENVER WEATHER

Lows: January, average low   16°F
Highs: July, average high   89°F
Average humidity: 38%
Average Annual Precipitation: 15″
Most annual rainfall: 23″
Most precipitation in 24 hrs: 6.5″

Mountain temperatures can be 10°- 30° cooler and 1″ per 1000 feet wetter. The record snowfall in Denver was 37.6″ on December 4-5, 1913. Weather buffs will want to visit the **National Center for Atmospheric Research** at 1850 Table Mesa Drive in Boulder or call for a reservation at the **National Earthquake Information Center** in Golden.

Our snowiest months often occur in the spring. If you're lucky enough to have a home near older trees, trim around the power lines or be prepared to be out of service. Investing in a generator might help. Getting quick service from our utility company (which literally took Public Service out of its name) can be like seeking service from our phone company. It's a never ending "quest."

Ski Season or Snow Place Like Home

Or how to spend lots of money to look fabulous in uncomfortable gear while waiting in long lines to take a tumble. Guess you can tell I'm not much of a skier. But many NATIVES are, and they squeal with sheer delight at the first report of snow in the mountains. I am told a powder day is better than sex! Just remember the best snow appears either on holidays with tons of tourists, or during the week, when you have to be at work. It rarely falls on weekends. The season usually kicks off after Thanksgiving and continues through April.

Skiing can be a deadly sport, as a couple of politicians found out. We now refer to running into a tree as "pulling a Bono." And Colorado looses about six folks every year to avalanches, usually because they are skiing outside the boundaries of the ski resorts. Even seasoned skiers are wearing helmets these

EXPERIENCE DOESN'T COUNT

Buddy Werner, a skier with incredible potential, died at age twenty-eight in a European avalanche. Mount Werner near his home town of Steamboat Springs is named in his honor. You can thank him for the skin tight slacks used by many ski enthusiasts.

days. Instead of looking out below, NATIVES know to look above for snow, falling rock and out of control downhill skiers.

To pass as a NATIVE you must know the difference between snowboarding and alpine, cross-country (Nordic) and telemark skiing. If you snowplow, you belong on the bunny hill, not on a bowl or mogul. And never ask to pet a snowcat.

Trust me, diehard skiers think of winter as a very slalom occasion.

MAJOR SKI RESORTS
(by skiable acres)

Vail	5160
Aspen/Snowmass Area	3683
Steamboat/Howelsen	3009
Winter Park/Mary Jane	2886
Copper	2433
Breckenridge	2043
Keystone/A-Basin	2100
Telluride	1700
Beaver Creek	1625
Wolf Creek	1600
Silverton	1600
Loveland	1365
Durango/Purgatory	1200
Crested Butte	1058
Eldora	680
Monarch	670
Powderhorn	510
Sunlight	460
SolVista (Silvercreek)	406
Ski Cooper	400

There are no friends on a powder day.

Other Seasons

Miller Moth Season dawns with the spring and can reappear in the fall. These annoying, dusty, but harmless creatures sneak into your house and go berserk bouncing off the sides of lampshades. The rest of the spring you'll spend washing their carcasses off walls and ceilings. The good thing is they aren't the kind of moths that eat clothing.

Hail Season, which lasts from March through October, comes at the first sign of a cracked windshield. You know you are a NATIVE when your car begins to resemble a large dimpled golf ball. You will average about one insurance claim every seven years for hail damage. Although June has the highest frequency of storms, the record breaker was the hail storm of July 1990, after which practically every home owner in Denver got a new roof. It cost an estimated $625 million in damages.

Summer, aka **Fire Season**, starts out hot and dry. And just when you think you can't take the heat, it gets hotter. Summers in Denver used to include the **Monsoon Season** when afternoon rains cooled things off. It has not happened in recent years and for this reason even true blue NATIVES are installing air conditioning in their homes.

When asked how to prevent forest fires after our "nuclear winter" (thank you Governor Owens for ruining the 2002 tourist season) someone suggested marriage counseling for all forest service personnel. If you recall the largest fire in Colorado history was set by a forest ranger, who used a letter from her estranged husband as kindling.

Tornados are rare for Denver, and are more likely to occur on the plains. Lightning strikes are common. It is best to get off the tee or down the fourteener to avoid summer afternoon storms. Rain originating from snow-covered mountain tops is cold no matter what the season, so be prepared to add another layer of clothing. In the Midwest the temperature difference from sun to shade is negligible. Here it can make a big difference. Seek out a cottonwood tree and a cool drink.

Aspen Viewing Season occurs in mid-to-late September and is more popular for NATIVES than tourists, who have to get their kids 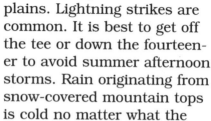 back home and in school by Labor Day. This is also the season when ranchers paint the word COW on their livestock, so hunters won't kill their profits.

Then comes **Bronco Season** when you see many people wearing orange, but at least it's not on top of their head and in the shape of a dairy product. All true NATIVES support the Broncos win or lose.

Springtime is one of the prettiest times of the year and can start as early as February. Intermittent snow storms remind you that it is indeed still winter and snow can fall as late as Memorial Day. For mountain folks these snow showers and winter run off are referred to as **Mud Season**.

Many states claim the adage, "If you don't like the weather wait a minute." Colorado NATIVES know just how true these words can be. As proof, the blizzards of 1885-86 killed so many cattle that sheep dominated the livestock raising in Colorado for the next fifty years. There's a memorial near the Kansas border at Towner to five frozen children and their bus driver. They were surprised by a seventy-five mile per hour blizzard that plunged the temperature to thirty-one degrees below zero on March 27, 1931. The June 1965 flood split Denver in two with many bridges gone or impassable. This flood effected twenty-seven counties and cost $102 million and ten lives. Our most recent record storm occurred in March 2003, when Denver International Airport's indestructible teflon-coated fiberglass ceiling finally ripped. It was put to the ultimate test, when close to thirty inches of snow fell and tested us all.

Tiny Bubbles Make You Warm All Over

What Colorado lacks in ocean waves, she more than makes up for in her bubbling hot springs. Understandably these areas were among the last that the Ute Indians gave up. It's hard to explain the euphoria you feel as you soak in a hot springs. If it's snowing, the flakes touch your face in tiny moist butterfly kisses that refresh and stun at the same time. Evenings are best, whether you're bedazzled by the snowflakes or the stars.

There are over thirty springs that currently welcome guests. No two look the same, and while swimsuits are the norm, clothing is often optional. A water temperature of at least ninety degrees qualifies them as a hot springs. In Colorado the hottest one is near Mount Princeton and, before diluted, comes in at 182°F.

The most renown spa resort is Glenwood Springs. Isaac Cooper used it to get away from mining with its many labor-intensive pains. He founded the town and proclaimed the healing powers of the water. James Crawford built a bathhouse at Steamboat Springs. The chugging riverboat sounds of the water gave the town its name.

Even though the "steamboat" spring namesake did not survive, the town and other springs in it have.

Spas must have seemed like life savers to early immigrants from the East coast. They had gotten used to the disease-ridden, populated cities with their open sewers and unfiltered water. Those who came to Colorado for their health were attracted to these seemingly curative waters. Popular through the turn of the century, spas lost favor during the Depression. Those that did survive did so by adding motels for the newly-mobile auto travelers that came after WWII.

For those of you who aren't used to getting into hot water, here are a few warnings. Check with your doctor before soaking, if you have high blood pressure or heart disease. Don't let your little ones get overheated in the pools. Don't drink the water and don't get in one if you see something green growing inside. If you're light-headed it's a sign to get out. This is a case where more may not be better for you.

Spas without attached hotels can be remote, rustic and difficult to find. The atmosphere is often like a private club for nature lovers. For most, it's best to stick with the well-known springs and leave the rustic spas to those of us who like going NATIVE.

History 101

Colorado means red, brownish red or colored red. Red in Spanish is rojo or colorado. Having nothing to be embarrassed about, one might assume the color refers to either the Native Americans or the red rocks scattered throughout the state. Actually it was the color of the river that gave both the state and river its name.

The Anasazi and Ute Indians are familiar to most NATIVES. Other tribes from Colorado include the Arapaho and Cheyenne, who fought with the Comanche and Kiowa, and the Ute and Apache, who fought with the Navajo. After a smallpox epidemic in 1839, there was some peace among the tribes.

All this came before the 1859 gold rush. In fact, Cherokee from Georgia were part of the Ralston party that discovered gold at Clear Creek in Arvada, a Denver suburb. They went on to California when the gold panned out. Then a man named Russell, with his Cherokee wife and fifty of her people, heard of Ralston's discovery and came to the Pike's Peak region. Within eight years of the discovery of gold most Indians were banished to Oklahoma. The Ute prevailed, but steadily lost lands until they were sent to Utah and southwestern Colorado in 1881.

I wonder if the American Indian sees the irony in today's West. The descendants of settlers, who took the Indian lands, are now feeling a similar pinch as wealthy city slickers take over the rural West. These city dwellers build huge palaces and want all the amenities of civilization from golf courses to shopping centers–everything they came here to escape. NATIVES are growing restless and penniless by comparison. Is this karma?

INFAMOUS SAND CREEK

In 1864 John Chivington from Glorietta Pass fame attacked a peaceful band of Ute Indians, mutilating 200 of them. The Indians went to Sand Creek believing it was safe and even displayed a white flag in peace. Chivington was later forced to resign, but not before going on stage to dramatize his killings. The movie Soldier Blue was based on the Sand Creek Massacre.

Much of Colorado's Anglo history and image is linked to the 1858-59 gold rush. The legendary Pike's Peak or Bust discovery near present day Colorado Springs is perhaps better known to non-NATIVES, than the gold discovered in Denver at the same time. In case NATIVES forget the importance of mining, they may turn to the state capitol building with its 24-karat gold leaf dome.

Even though we like to look at the West as the land of rugged individualism, big business and the government played a vital role in its development. The government gave railroads land for building track and gave large ranchers land for open or free-range grazing. Smelter owners controlled mining, since surface gold quickly panned out. Thus, most small time prospectors stayed that way. Not unlike the business climate today.

Colorado was not part of the Transcontinental Railroad of 1869. In reality this route only went from Omaha to Sacramento via Cheyenne, Wyoming, which provided easier access through the Rockies. The first truly transcontinental train came about a year later with the Kansas Pacific Railroad through Strasburg and then into Denver. Spurs were built to Denver from the Cheyenne main line, since Denver was the supply hub for the miners, farmers and ranchers.

Colorado reached statehood in 1876 and was nicknamed the Centennial State. (America was one hundred years old at the time.) The silver rush began a year later in Leadville. When silver was cast aside by the US government in favor of the gold standard, it spurred the 1893 depression. The value and demand for silver plummeted and ruined many.

At the turn of the century during Mayor Speer's reign (1904-1918) the city of Denver became the

MISSION IMPOSSIBLE

All NATIVES know the Tabor saga. Senator Horace Tabor cast aside his wife for the youthful Baby Doe. He was ruined by the 1893 depression and died. His last words to her were to keep the Matchless Mine. Taking him literally, she lived at the mine site near Leadville for over thirty-five years until she went nuts and froze to death. One daughter was killed in a flop house in Chicago and the other "disavowed any knowledge of their actions." You can still visit the Baby Doe mine.

"City Beautiful." Although part of a political machine resembling Mayor Daley's Chicago, Speer introduced color with trees, a park system, paved streets and a plan that even today 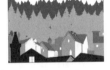 makes Denver one of the greenest cities in America. Many find it hard to believe that Denver had no trees when it was first settled.

WWII brought another boom to Colorado after the Dust Bowl and Depression of the 1930s. NATIVES forget the build up after Pearl Harbor, when the government realized Colorado's unique position away from vulnerable coastlines. That attack galvanized the government into a glacial age of ground breaking glorification. The Federal Center, the Arsenal, Rocky Flats, Lowry Air Force Base, Buckley Field, Fitzsimons, NORAD, the Air

Force Academy and Peterson Air Force Base made Colorado the second largest government depository outside Washington, DC.

GI's, returning from WWII, accelerated the building boom. We continued our exploitation of natural resources throughout the 50s and 60s. Although mining was on a decline, water became an even more precious commodity, as the government persisted in constructing countless dams and reservoirs.

Luckily for us there grew an equally demanding environmental movement during this time. It came to a head in the early 1970s, when Colorado finally said enough and rejected the invitation to host the 1976 Olympics. Growth, environmental concerns and reports of financial losses from other Olympics were the reasons. The voting public may also have been confused. The ballet issue was worded in the tricky manner we've become famous for, where no means you're for the initiative and yes means you're against it. Thus, we go down in history as the only city, state or nation that ever rejected the games after they were awarded.

Heck, we didn't even complete Interstate 70, through Colorado until 1992. The reasons were environmental concerns for Glenwood Canyon and the engineering challenge caused by the mountains. It was worth the wait.

DO IT TILL YOU GET IT RIGHT

Enos Abijah Mills (1870-1922) came to Colorado at fourteen for his health. While working as a cowboy, he delivered some cattle to a rancher named Lamb at the base of Long's Peak. By 1888 he became a professional guide to its summit and climbed it 297 times! He bought Lamb's property, gave up guiding to operate his hotel there and wrote sixteen books on Colorado's wildlife. His obsession to preserve the area, resulted in the formation of the Colorado Mountain Club, which is still in existence. Their primary goal was the creation of Rocky Mountain National Park. That goal came to fruition on September 4, 1915, helped in part by a conservationist president. Adjacent to the park stands the (Teddy) Roosevelt National Forest.

By the late 1980s the government building reversed itself and now many of the facilities are gone, downsized or converted to other uses. You may still order all those helpful brochures from the Federal Citizen Information Center in Pueblo, however. It's what put Pueblo on the map for many.

Modern Colorado often centers on the doings of its largest city, except when Georgetown politics makes the news. Denver is trying to shun its cow town image. In fact it's trying to become the kind of city we all moved away from. It can now proudly claim the new Denver International Airport, baggage and all. Costing $4.8 billion in 1995, people still complain about the time it takes to get out there. Despite the vagaries of the weather and our thin air, the airport has been successful where it counts–arriving and departing safely. You get an idea of how far away from Denver the airport is, when you mistake the roof peaks on the terminal for the distant mountains.

Denver is unique. Where else would citizens support the building of an aquarium in a semiarid climate and fight for its survival during a drought? Or get fooled into taxing ourselves for the privilege of new baseball, basketball and football stadiums, while the owners and players laugh all the way to the bank? These government handouts to select businesses are counter to what I think is our NATIVE entrepreneurial spirit. Are there shoe boxes full of money or deceased voters in our future? You Illinois folks know what I'm talking about.

Denver's brewpub-owning mayor is stirring things up by requiring city and county employees to earn their raises through a merit system. What a concept! And he promises less confrontation between the county and business owners. As a "fellow" scooterer, the mayor is OK in my book.

From Ancient Sites to Ghost Towns

Ancient history is a relative term. In Colorado fossils reveal important steps in both plant and animal evolution. Archeological sites also count as modern day tourist attractions for NATIVES and non-NATIVES alike. Many are stunned to find dinosaur bones older than Strom Thurmond's. From pre-man to Century 21® man, the state offers many opportunities to explore our origins.

I CAN DIG IT

Dinosaur Ridge contains dinosaur footprints and an interpretive trail. Go west through the Denver suburbs on Alameda Parkway and turn right a quarter mile past C-470.

Dinosaur National Monument in northwest Colorado is near Dinosaur on Highway 40. It has an amazing display of dinosaur bones embedded in a wall. Great scenery is nearby.

Picket Wire Canyonlands, twenty miles south of La Junta on Highway 109 and County Road 802, has 1300 dinosaur footprints. Take bikes, water and food, since it is over 5 miles to the tracks and camping isn't allowed.

Rabbit Valley is 30 miles west of Grand Junction at Exit 2 off I-70. It has 30 species of dinosaurs on 286 acres. There are guided digs.

Garden Park Quarry is eight miles north of Cañon City on Red Canyon and Garden Park Roads. Most natural history museums in the US have bones from this site.

Florissant Fossil Beds. If you are into prehistoric plants instead of animals this is the place for you. Nothing sleeps on these beds, except petrified stumps. West of Pike's Peak on highway 24, this site has a human timeline giving you a humbling perspective of our short tenure here on earth.

Pawnee Buttes. If you want to know what quiet sounds like, before children were invented, check out these 300-foot sandstone hills and surrounding grasslands. East of Fort Collins in the middle of nowhere is the home to many fossils and birds. James Michener's book Centennial referred to this area as Rattlesnake Buttes. High top shoes are a good idea, as is a wide angle camera.

The Great Sand Dunes are tucked between the Sangre de Cristo and San Juan Mountains northeast of Alamosa. The largest sand box you'll ever play in, dunes reach over 700 feet high. There's a surprise for you if you go during spring run off. Medano Creek meanders in front of the dunes along with a few mule deer. Stomping through water in a desert seems like an environmental oxymoron.

Mesa Verde. NATIVES should visit the Anasazi cliff houses in the off season to avoid wild fires and the even wilder tourists, who forget all about sharing the road in an effort not to miss anything, except, if you're lucky, your car. The Anasazi Heritage Center at 27501 Highway 184 in Dolores is a starting point. Remember that paintings are pictographs and carvings are petroglyphs.

FAUX DWELLINGS

An alternative to Mesa Verde are the Manitou Springs Cliff Dwellings west of Colorado Springs on highway 24. Around 1907 the artifacts were pilfered from Indian sites over 300 miles away. The dwelling itself was hauled there in pieces by train at a cost of $100,000.

Needless to say the history of Colorado is tied to its exploitable resources. Whether minerals, oil, water, natural gas, cheap grazing, sprawling suburbs or treasures of nature, it is up to us to police ourselves and take care of what we still consider part of the American lore and lure.

Part of that lure includes gunfights and ghost towns. Send visitors to see a corny, but spirited gunfight at Buckskin Joe's or take a drive along Clear Creek off Highway 24 on county road 390 to visit ghost and mining towns. Many older dwellings were salvaged, relocated and can now be seen at South Park City in Fairplay.

SNAKE, RATTLE & ROLL

North of Fort Lupton in 1925 Katherine Slaughterback went out to hunt dinner. She saw a rattlesnake and shot it. More came and she clubbed them. They kept coming. Two hours later Rattlesnake Kate had killed 140 snakes! She skinned them and made a dress.

The Local Cuisine

In my opinion, never eat at Casa Bonita without an excuse. Use the one we all do–visitors with children. Even though the short-lived Rain Forest chain came close, nothing beats the tantalizing tackiness of Casa Bonita. Although fun for a four year old, it is embarrassing for NATIVES, whose visitors think they're actually tasting authentic Mexican food by going there.

I'M STUFFED

If you want critter meat, like deer, buffalo, antelope, elk or the infamous Rocky Mountain oysters, go to The Buckhorn Exchange, owner of Denver's first liquor license. Where else can you see animal faces stuffed on the walls, while you stuff them in your face?

Needless to say most Mexican cuisine in Colorado is excellent and can be priced all over the board. Polenta is now put on menus as if it were a delicacy. For those of you who don't know, it is cornmeal mush or porridge. Oliver Twist would feel right at home.

True NATIVES should be able to bite into a chili pepper without shedding a tear. Gringos should carry tissues just in case. For NATIVES, peppers, which are high in vitamin C, are the "sniffling, sneezing, aching so you can rest medicine." Eating them should clear out any sinus problems. Remember to ask for salsa or picante, not ketchup. In authentic Mexican restaurants start with red, milder chili sauces and work your way up to the hotter green (verde) ones.

Take 2 and call me in the morning

Although ranching is alive and well in Colorado, so are vegetarians. They have boldly inserted vegetables and fruit into our meaty diet! There is often a vegetarian alternative on restaurant menus.

Do not let the fancy names and high prices fool you. Finding a good reasonably-priced restaurant with generous portions at mountain resorts, is like trying to ski uphill. I'm more often frustrated than pleased. For consistency and pre-dictable pricing try fast food. For a truly good dinner in the mountains ccok your own in your condo or go out and be willing to spend a bundle. Try a recommendation from the local Chamber of Commerce.

It is far easier to list the types of food we don't have in Denver. Let's see there's . . .

WINING INSTEAD OF DINING

California...Schmalifornia. Colorado boasts it's own Wine Country from Palisade, east of Grand Junction to Montrose along Highway 50. Tour the vineyards by bike near the Colorado River.

THE COLFAX EXPERIENCE

The Satire Lounge at 1920 Colfax in
Denver has been around since the
1960s. Now a Mexican restaurant, they
once hosted the Smothers Brothers,
who lived in an apartment above the
bar. Judy Collins also sang there.

And just because I knew you
would ask, the Denver omelet did
originate here and includes green
peppers, onions and ham. The
addition of cheese makes for a
Western omelette. Don't forget to
try the Rocky Mountain Oysters, a
delicacy in more ways than one–so
much so that few NATIVES have
tried them.

Eating out is a way of life these
days. Maybe because the growing
season here is so short. If you're a
gardener, you're in for a challenge,
especially in the mountains. Herbs
do well, but it is seldom that a
tomato turns red before the
first frost kills the green ones.
Maybe growing water-conserv-
ing plants should be called
xero-scaping, instead of
xeriscaping.

FOOD FOR THOUGHT

Killing germs takes longer here, since
water boils at 202° F in Denver, instead
of 212°F at sea level. Thus cook your
food longer. And use less yeast, baking
soda and/or powder when baking.

Don't Worry, Be Healthy

Although fat is where it's at in America today, thin is still in in Colorado. Health awareness does show, since Colorado has fewer obese people than the rest of America, with the exception of maybe Hollywood. Even pedestrians keep in good shape by dodging cars.

To pass as a healthy NATIVE enjoy a workout at one of our sun-filled playgrounds. Avoid popular tourist spots and check out bike shops in the mountains. There you can eavesdrop on the best single track locations in the area. These same stores often have information on local hiking and other activities, you may not find in the big city.

EXERCISE FOR YOUR BRAIN

For detailed USGS maps try one of Denver's favorite spectator sports, browsing at Tattered Cover Book Store. But be careful, once you start looking around in there you may forget all about the great outdoors.

To give you an idea of how NATIVES like to exercise, there are over 130 bike trails just in the Denver Metro area. They meander from Boulder in the north to Parker in the south and from Golden in the west to Aurora in the east. There are charity runs and walks for everyone from cancer survivors to dog lovers. And the latter can often be seen evenings and weekends, stretching their legs with their canine pets, usually a golden retriever. If cats would let us, we'd walk them, too.

We've also banned smoking in some areas to the betterment of NATIVES and forests. Bans are in effect in Boulder, Pueblo, Fort Collins, Aspen and other smaller communities. You can still smoke in Denver, but your chimney can't on those winter days when the brown cloud hovers overhead. To control pollution, weather reports include Red Advisories to indicate a no burn day, and Blue Advisories to say go ahead and use the fireplace.

Colorado used to be the place to get cured, when it came to disease. More than one in three Denverites before WWI moved here for relief from tuberculosis. Today the state still ranks low in deaths from cancer, heart disease and homicides. It is inexplicably high, though, like other Western states, in the rate of suicides.

And while insects in Texas qualify as pet size, Colorado's bugs are smaller and often more deadly. Rocky Mountain spotted fever comes from ticks. Red spots develop after a high fever and headache. Antibiotics tend to mediate the danger. Given the flu epidemic and the 2002-2004 West Nile virus outbreak, you might think moving here isn't a good idea. NATIVES won't mind if you come just to visit. Other deterrents are that Colorado has a higher incidence of skin cancer (always higher when closer to the sun) and multiple sclerosis (always higher the farther away from the equator). Although lower birth weight is associated with high altitude, more often it results from multiple births, smoking or not gaining enough weight during pregnancy.

When NATIVES aren't exercising, we're working hard on medical research, raising and eating organically grown foods and using the latest herbal remedies. As health aware as we are, it's ironic we have such a poor showing when it comes to immunizing our own children.

FAITH HEALERS

Aimee Semple McPherson was a Canadian farm girl turned evangelist and healer. She converted 12,000 to her Los Angeles based Foursquare Gospel Church during her visit to Denver in 1921. She was the first woman to receive an FCC radio license and was known as religion's P.T. Barnum. She killed herself in 1944 at the age of 54, but her church lives on.

Francis Schlatter returned to Denver, from healing the poor in New Mexico, at the bidding of a politician in 1895. Opportunists soon began selling items, including their places in line, to those who came to be healed. He left in disgust. Schlatter never took money from those he tried to help. Even hard core reporters couldn't explain away his healing powers. Where he went after leaving Denver remains a mystery.

There's Coffee and then There's Coffee.

Back in 1982 you couldn't find a place to get a late night cup of coffee and bagels seemed exotic. Now even the police have vacated the donut holes for bagel holes.

Seriously though folks, nothing like a little caffeine to get you in the mood for the morning commute. Beware of drivers who have a double (espresso, that is). My theory is that road rage started about the same time espresso became popular.

Some of the more entrepreneurial NATIVES have as much regard for Starbucks® as they do for Bill Gates. But you have to admire the marketing tactics. We haven't seen this kind of brainwashing, since four wheel drives became a necessity. How did we manage in the snow before SUVs came along? And how did we ever dare make coffee at home, when for just twelve times as much we can now wait in line for it?

I also blame coffee houses for the tipping craze. People who serve me at my table and keep me happy get a tip. Here's a tip for you coffee makers: drink tea, it's healthier. I'm even thinking of creating a set of cards with tips on them to hand out in lieu of money:

- A penny saved is a penny earned.

- One in my hand is worth two in your tip jar . . .

Having said that, there are independent coffee roasters that serve coffee with an appealing ambiance, which you may like more than your home brew. Whether it is coffee or another product, help out NATIVES and the local economy and ABC–Always Buy Colorado. It should be ABN, wouldn't you agree?

HOME PLATE

Yet another idea from the proud, the few, the Coloradan:

Even though it is no longer being issued, at one time you could get this limited edition license plate to promote products raised or manufactured in Colorado. The cost was $35.00. What's hugs and kisses got to do with it? Perhaps that's why it fell out of favor.

There's Water and then There's Water.

As mentioned, we live in a semiarid state. So do your part. Conserve water by planting non-NATIVE flowers and bushes and shrink the lawn to nothing. This xeriscaping will allow the cities to permit builders to construct more housing so more people can use more water. Thus your conservation efforts result in urban sprawl. Do you feel better now?

It wasn't any better in the old days, when the government gave away land and built dams on all the rivers to irrigate the farms. This was so successful that the government had to buy up and store all the excess commodities. They ended up paying the farmers not to plant and built more expensive water diversion projects for ex-farmers who moved to the city for jobs. It makes you wonder why we ruined the natural course of our rivers in the first place.

ARTESIAN WELLS

In 1900 Denver had about 150 artesian wells, the deepest over 1000 feet. The Brown Palace still uses one. The pressure from one building's well was so strong, it ran that building's elevators. The organ in the Trinity United Methodist Church was powered by a water wheel from a well. The natural pressure is gone now and pumps must be used to get the water flowing.

So how did we get to this point? The early Indians irrigated. The southern Spanish settlers learned their irrigating principles from the Moors. Early farming attempts near Pueblo in 1787 and at Bent's Fort in 1832 failed because the Indians were restless, although their horses enjoyed munching on the few crops that did succeed. By 1859 much of the San Luis Valley was irrigated with about forty ditches.

European farmers settling in northern Colorado often began as communes. The best known was the Union Colony at Greeley. They ended up paying twenty times their estimate for irrigation, because they didn't know what they were doing. Other colonies "cropped up" near water sources in Fort Collins, in Longmont, and in Dearfield, an all-Black 1910 settlement. Cotopaxi was a short-lived Jewish farm colony begun in 1882. After farming became passè, groups switched to political and religious colonies. Nucla, founded in 1904, was a socialist experiment. Crestone in the 1980s was mystical with crystals and temples, but I digress.

The British were happy to help invest in irrigation. They bought up railroad land, built ditches on it and then sold it for twenty-five times the original price.

Colorado pioneered the idea of sharing water. As early as 1861 the state instituted the doctrine of appropriation, which meant that no one person owned the water on his land. Rather they owned the right to take from the water source whatever they needed for daily use and then leave the rest for others. Thus your neighbor could dig a ditch through your property to irrigate his land.

Cities also dug their own ditches and wells and later used canals for distribution. The Smith Ditch, which still supplies water for the lakes at Washington Park and City Park in Denver, is an example. By 1905 the animal waste in the South Platte River was so bad that Denver sought a better storage facility for their fresh water. Cheesman Dam was the world's highest gravity arch dam and deepest reservoir when it was built.

Even though most of us live on the Eastern Slope, much of our water comes from diversion projects that bring water from the Western Slope. Agriculture still uses the majority of the water that doesn't evaporate, with residential use at only five percent. So be prepared to have a rock garden and think twice about installing a sprinkler system under current watering restrictions.

NATIVES begrudgingly do their part to conserve water every time they go to the bathroom. I wish I had invested in plungers when toilet tanks were reduced from ten gallons of water to just one and a half. I'd sure be a lot more flush than I am now.

Political Graph

If you're Republican, you should fit right into Colorado politics. However, Denver, like many large cities, is an island of liberalism surrounded by an ocean of conservatives. Using this analogy we might deduce that the conservatives are all wet. . . In spite of political affiliations, you will find that many of us are independents. as shown by recent amendments that give us more say on how our tax money is used.

The Governor and legislature must pass a balanced budget. When they can't, they issue more tickets and install more parking meters. Two psuedo taxes include the fee you pay for your car's emission test and, if you're not careful, the parking tickets you get from city street cleaners the first week of every month. New fees for businesses also appear, such as paying for fire inspections that were once free. This money gets thrown into the general fund and seldom finds its way to the cause for which it was created.

To fight back voters passed The Bruce and Tabor Amendments. The former lets us vote for or against tax increases. You'd think it would always be no, but incredibly that's not the case. The TABOR Amendment (Taxpayer's Bill of Rights) forbids the state from keeping excess revenue. These two amendments are the common excuses for our budget crunch. I'm sure many of us would reconsider the Tabor Amendment, if we got back something in return. I might give up Tabor for the right to vote on salary increases for state senators and representatives.

Entrepeneurs should know the Secretary of State's office. This is where you submit your new business name (don't forget the mountain logo). And it's where you get licensed and sign up to pay for all those special taxes. The state has an agency to meet your every need, if you don't mind being put on hold or the e-mail equivalent.

LEAK LAWS

In 1974 women finally were free to pee without paying a fee at the old Stapleton Airport. It seems the city got in trouble, because the men were not charged for this privelege. Unable to figure out how to put meters on men's urinals, half of the women's pay toilets were removed. All are free to pee at the new airport.

As a NATIVE, you will hear references to and should be familiar with the following past and present politicians:

Governor Owens: A leader who admits to reading books, Mr. Bill is naive in thinking that capital punishment is a deterrent. Next he's going to tell us poor minorities have the same chance of winning a jury trial as a rich white one.

State Senator Gary Hart: If he'd gone on *60 Minutes* and declared his philandering, would he also be an ex-president by now?

Governor Lamm: Colorado's answer to Dr. Kevorkian, perhaps he is why people prefer Florida and Arizona for retirement. Now that he's getting up there in age, does he feel it is his civic *duty to die*?

Senator Ben Nighthorse Campbell: Here's a true Westerner–part Native American, part Easy Rider, part Democrat, part Republican all mixed into one.

Reporter: Knock! Knock!
Senator Pat Schroeder: Who's there?
Reporter: Boo.
Senator Pat Schroeder: Boo who?
Reporter: Female Presidential Candidate Can't Control Emotions

Mayor Peña: His key to success was getting 6000 new Hispanic registered voters. Got citizenship? He's living proof that if you build a four billion dollar airport, they will come and make you Secretary of Transportation.

Mayor Webb: Thanks for giving American history students a current example of the spoils system.

Thanks also to a little known judge named Benjamin Lindsey, who in 1903 created a juvenile court separating young offenders from hardened criminals. It became the model for a national system. He also believed in trial marriages and sex education and wrote a book exposing political corruption. Too liberal for Colorado during the Klu Klux Klan revival of the 1920s, he moved to California in 1928.

The key thing to remember when voting in Colorado is to read everything carefully. When politicians haven't done their job to get the message across, when the language is unclear, when you're not sure what you're voting on or when there are a lot of double negatives or run on sentences like this one, Just Vote No.

WATER POLITICS

A farm boy, who lived most of his life in Palisade near the Colorado River, Wayne Aspinall was a teacher before he got into politics. He served in the state house and senate. In 1948 at fifty-three he became a US congressman, focusing his career in two areas-land and water use. He believed in "mining" the rivers and public lands as commodities and was the most powerful influence on the Colorado River basin. In the 50s and 60s, he pushed through over forty water projects, including the Glen Canyon Dam, the Blue Mesa Dam on the Gunnison River and the Fryingpan-Arkansas diversion. By 1966 the harmful effects of daming the rivers began to emege. That, budget concerns and the environmental movement, which Aspinall attacked, made him appear out of touch. He lost his 1972 re-election bid and died in Palisade eleven years later.

Unheeded Laws

Here are some laws you should ignore, as do the rest of the NATIVES.

Catapults may not be fired at buildings in Aspen. This same law prohibits throwing snowballs. They are probably afraid you'll ruin their fur coats. It is best to leave that to tree huggers and animal rights folks.

In Boulder you can insult a cop until he tells you to stop. Only then does it become illegal. Instead of a law, wouldn't it be better to just have a special day, like Insult Your Local Police Day? Get it out of your system and then hold your tongue the rest of the year.

It is illegal to mistreat rats in Denver, but picking on the home-less is AOK. It's also acceptable to feed wild animals. Just don't act appalled, when they break into your property looking for food and then have to be shot.

Not only is it embarrassing to fall while skiing, but in Vail it is illegal to ski into any of their equipment, such as lift towers or signs. It is much better to let another skier or tree break your fall. And don't try hanging a clothesline in Vail either.

Current Colorful Denver Characters

Every city has its share of commercially unappealing folks. No exceptions here. For many NATIVES the mention of Jabs, Kacey, Shane, Rocky or O'Meara bring up visions of wild animals, birthday sales, nasal monotony, tackiness and Texas drawl, respectively. But the most irritating thing about these local business people is that sooner or later you'll end up shopping in at least one of their stores.

Musical local characters include Hazel Miller, an under-appreciated blues singer; Lannie Garrett, stylized entertainment; Nelson Rangel, Denver's answer to the squeaking sax, aka Kenny G; and Opie Gone Bad, a rock funk band heard at home hockey games. Alas, Denver's namesake John Denver is no more, but his Rocky Mountain High lives on in all of us. Other characters of culture include cowboy poet Baxter Black and John Fielder, a good nature photographer and even better marketer. Black and white photography purists prefer Hal Gould's Camera Obscura Gallery. Knowing these cultural icons will help you pass as a NATIVE. You can read all about the Best of Denver in Patricia Calhoun's Westword–one of many alternative newspapers or visit the Golden Triangle galleries in Denver on the First Friday of every month.

Ignored but Not Forgotten

Colorado's attraction remains its myth of rugged individualism. The lottery is our way of panning for gold. Consumption of goods is now up there with exploitation of natural resources. News entertainment and history extol the virtues of the successful and the wealthy. Here are a few, who went against the odds, and came to help the not-so-successful.

CASIMIRO BARELA

A New Mexico immigrant, Barela came to Colorado to start a farm near Trinidad. He expanded into sheep and cattle ranching and eventually became one of the three richest stockmen in Colorado before entering politics. He printed papers in Spanish to keep his congressional constituency informed and acted as a kind of Denver ambassador to Mexico. He defended Hispanic landowners, when their ownership was threatened by the discovery of coal in southern Colorado and switched parties in 1901 to support Roosevelt's popular reform movement. He served in the state senate from 1876 to 1916, one of the longest tenures in US history.

DOC SUSIE ANDERSON

Twenty-five percent of Susan Anderson's graduating class in 1897 were women. Doctoring then was dirty, thankless and unprofitable. When new cures brought prestige and better earnings, it became unsuitable for women. Doc Susie never made much money on her practice. She came to Fraser to recoup from tuberculosis. Her patients included Scandinavian lumberjacks, who later built her a home and office. Her fear of being robbed kept her from using drugs on her patients. She lectured them about cleanliness and nutrition. She made her rounds with a gun and her small dog and got around by snowshoe and train. She brought serious cases to Denver General, humbling new interns and catching up on the latest procedures. In 1926 she became Grand County Coroner during the building of the Moffat Tunnel and in 1939 treated broken bones at the new Winter Park ski area. She never owned a horse, a phone or a car and served the Fraser area till she was 88, two years before she died.

DAVID DAY

At 18 David Day won the Congressional Medal of Honor. After the Civil War he wandered to Missouri, where he learned to write, opened a shop and declared bankrupcy by age 30. He went west to Ouray in 1880 and started his own newspaper, the *Solid Muldoon*. In 1882 he moved it to Durango. His journalism, unlike other newspapers of the time, took the side of the people. He despised mine owners that came, saw, stripped clean and then sold off what was left, abandoning both towns and lives in their wake. And he fought rail owners, who held a city hostage for high freight rates under the threat of abandoning them altogether. Lawsuits were frequent and he found himself writing many an article behind bars. Day named the *Muldoon* after a fighter, who lost every fight, but never quit. Day continued his fight until he died in 1914.

Colorful Colorado Critters

Although there are plenty of fish and gunslinger stories, here are some tall tales all NATIVES should know. Critters include burros, a headless chicken, dogs and the Teddy bear.

Prunes the burro worked just about every mine in the Fairplay area for sixty-two years with his human partner Rupe Sherwood. Although preferring to pan, tough times forced Rupe to work the underground mines and Prunes got to be known by all the miners. When Rupe was too old to spend his winters in Fairplay, the community took care of old Prunes. During a great blizzard he became trapped in a shelter. He was so weak when they found him, everyone agree to put him down. People collected money for a memorial and a year later Rupe's ashes joined Prunes. You can visit the gravesite on Front Street in Fairplay.

Another burro named **Shorty** was the Fairplay pancake-loving town mooch. He had a sidekick, Bum the dog. When Shorty died and was buried on the courthouse lawn, Bum was so grieved that he laid on the grave, refused to eat and died. His bones were buried with Shorty.

The burro craze got out of hand, when in the 1930s Samuel D. Nicholson donated $250,000 for a monument to the essential pack animal and friend to miners! Luckily, this folly never occurred and the money was used instead for the Samuel D. Nicholson wing of the Denver General Hospital.

SAINTLY BEASTS OF BURDEN

Burros were and are indispensable pack animals. They eat almost anything and don't drink much. Legend says the burro, that carried Jesus on Palm Sunday, wanted to bare the burden of the cross. Symbolic lines that form a cross between its shoulders and down its back were its reward.

About the only thing not controversial about building the Boulder-Denver Turnpike back in 1952 was **Shep, the shepherd mix dog**. He sauntered in before the tollhouse was done and toll takers and motorists alike adopted him, contributing doggie treats and a fund for his upkeep. He stayed until his death in 1964. The road paid for itself thirteen years ahead of schedule. You can still see Shep's gravesite at the Broomfield exit–
Our Pal, Part Shepherd, Mostly Affection.

What can you say about **Mike, the headless chicken**, except that he ran around like a chicken with his head cut off? Mike's owner went out to kill dinner knowing his mother-in-law liked the neck. His skill with an ax and a fortunate blood clot left Mike headless, but still employable. He was fed with an eyedropper and went on tour, making $4500 a month. He porked out, gained over five pounds and lived for another year and a half. Mike's owners, appropriately enough, were from the town of Fruita.

Roy Rogers' horse Trigger was the model for **Bucky Bronco**, the horse/mascot you see rearing up in front of the new football stadium. Bucky is twenty-seven feet tall and weighs in at 1600 pounds. Finished in 1976, he moved to the newly-named Invesco Field at Mile High Stadium in 2001.

Perhaps the most famous critter NATIVES like to claim is the **Teddy bear**. Many know it was named after Teddy Roosevelt, but the real story is hard to get a bead on. One version is that his daughter Alice, while staying with her father in Glenwood Springs, saw a bear pelt and named it Teddy. Another story is that Glenwood Springs residents gave a toy bear to the President after a hunt nearby. A third tale is that after his first bear kill made headlines, a toy manufacturer made a small stuffed one and sent it to Alice. However, three years before his Glenwood Springs trip, a political cartoonist heard about Teddy's refusal to kill a bear cub that someone caught for him to shoot. His cartoon yielded the Teddy bear. Obviously NATIVES prefer the Glenwood Springs connection.

Close Encounters of the Natural Kind

Kids are a big reason to avoid popular tourist spots. Get them in the wild and their constant chattering scares off the wildlife, which parents take them to see. From wildflowers to wild animals, respect your non-human NATIVES. My closest encounter to a wild animal in Illinois was dodging an occasional deer on the road. But here in Colorado there have been many memorable encounters.

Hiking through a Fairplay neighborhood, I was stopped in my tracks by a lumbering skunk! They are usually seen as roadkill and most often smelled before seen. They're much larger alive and excite the *flight over fight* panic button when seen up close and personal.

While bicycling in Waterton Canyon, southwest of Metro Denver, the end of the road near the dam held quite a surprise. It was rutting season and two big-horned sheep were doing their version of a head on collision. The pop of their heads hitting one another echoed through the canyon and was very, very cool.

While camping at the Great Sand Dunes in southern Colorado, I was given the choice of a near-full campground or one popular with bears. I chose the latter, never saw a bear, but did enjoy the very mellow, big-eared mule deer.

And while soaking in a hot springs, the steam rose around a ghostly deer, as it strolled downhill along the hot water's source.

Nature lovers often feel ranchers are not paying their fare share for grazing on Bureau of Land Management (BLM) acreage. If cows would eat deadfall (the dead fallen trees in the forests), it would cut down on forest fires and we'd all be happier. But you can pay them now or pay them later at the grocery store. If you are really concerned and want to make a difference, eat buffalo.

WHICH CAME FIRST?

Today Colorado raises more chickens than cattle. After cattle comes pigs and then sheep.

When it comes to wildflowers, every NATIVE should be able to identify the bright orange Indian paintbrush, the blue and white columbine and the spike-leafed tall yucca plant. If you are hiking around the state, the pasque flower (a large fuzzy crocus), wild iris, blue penstemon, yellow potentilla bush, scarlet trumpet-like gilia, blue larkspur, lupine, white mariposa lily and yellow pea are plentiful and easy to identify. Do yourself a favor, get a field guide of wildflowers and impress the NATIVES.

TAME FLOWER GEMS

The **Betty Ford Alpine Garden** is my favorite thing in Vail and it's free. **Hudson Gardens** at 6115 South Santa Fe in Metro Denver is a great place for flower lovers of all ages. Swing in their Secret Garden and listen to the birds. Picknicking is acceptable. Flowers are not the only attraction at the **Denver Botanic Gardens**. Their summer concerts are great for picnics and music lovers. View flowers all summer long in many of Denver's over 200+ parks. Steamboat Springs also has many parks, but don't miss the charming **Yampa River Botanic Park** at the end of Pamela Lane.

Flowers aren't the only thing to watch. No self-respecting NATIVE can avoid taking photos of quaking aspens as they turn a spectacular golden yellow in the fall. Some trees get as large as eighteen inches in diameter and as high as eighty feet. They are one of the largest plants on earth, sending up hundreds of clones of themselves, which we see as separate trees.

WILD FLOWER GEMS

Crested Butte in northeast Colorado has a **Wildflower Festival** in early July that is well worth the trip. Another spectacular display appears along Engineer Pass, part of the **Alpine Loop** outside of Lake City. It is incredible and pristine.

Here's a natural law for all of you non-NATIVES: *It is illegal to willfully deface, disfigure, or injure beyond normal use any rocks, trees, shrubbery, wildflowers or other features of natural environment in the recreation areas of Colorado.*

That means tourists and children should not pick the flowers. And put those smelly butts out in your ashtray, not in the dry forest!

WILD ANIMAL VIEWING

Buffalo (2000 lbs) can be seen twenty miles west of Denver at I-70 near Genesee or near Grand Junction at the Colorado National Monument.

Moose (1000 lbs) appear at high mountain wetlands near a forest edge. See them in North Park surrounding Walden (150 miles northwest of Denver) in Larimer and Grand Counties. They were reintroduced to Colorado in 1978.

Elk (800 lbs) Spotting elk is easy in the town of Estes Park, along 285 just down the hill after Kenosha Pass or at Elk Meadow Park near Evergreen. Listen for their high-pitched bugle— wimpy for their size.

Bear (450 lbs) Black and brown bear (no grizzlies) range from the Foothills to the Western Slope. They are dormant from the end of November to March. If you see one calmly back away, keep facing it, but do not make eye contact or sudden movements.

Mule Deer (400 lbs; female 200 lbs)
Look for their big ears. Small ears
mean they are white-tailed deer. Both
are plentiful statewide.

Big Horn Sheep (280 lbs) Not that
common, they prefer grassy slopes
from 5000 (winter) to 8500 (summer)
feet in altitude. Try Waterton Canyon
southwest of Denver near Mt. Evans or
the slopes above Georgetown.

Mountain Goat (200 lbs) They are
easily seen above timberline especially
on top of Mt. Evans. They forage
at dawn and dusk and were
reintroduced to the state in 1947.

Antelope (150 lbs) Antelope or
pronghorn are spotted at dusk or late
afternoon in empty fields between
Jefferson and Fairplay along 285 and
along I-70 on the plains east of Denver.

Mountain Lion (130 lbs) Also called
cougar and puma, they prefer woods
and bushy areas over forests and
prairie. Do not run, crouch or turn your
back on one. Make yourself appear
large and throw things at it if attacked.

Beaver (55 lbs) You are more likely to
see beaver ponds than beaver. It takes
them 30 minutes to fell a 5 inch diameter tree. Wherever there is a stream,
you'll generally see their work.

Coyote (40 lbs) You are more likely to
hear than see one. They are
common, active at dawn and
dusk and vary in color from
gray to buff to red.

Fox (9-11 lbs) Red ones are found in woods and wetlands (Cherry Creek in Denver) and gray ones in canyons and foothills. Swift and kit foxes are smaller. Swifts are found on the eastern plains and kits in desert shrublands.

Marmot (11 lbs) They are seen mostly in alpine meadows but can live in the foothills. These brown fur balls look chubby and like to hang out on rocks to warm themselves, when they aren't hibernating or foraging for food.

Pika (less than $1/2$ lb) You are more likely to hear their shrill chirp first and then see them scurry near treeline rock piles or talus, in NATIVE-speak.

If you don't get a chance to get out in the wild, check out the local rodeo scene. County fairs in smaller towns often have rodeos for children, which are hilarious to watch. There's nothing quite like a little cowgirl with big red boots and a bandanna, galloping her stick pony around a small obstacle course. And you can't miss the mutton busting, when your favorite little buckaroo exchanges a hat for a helmet as he or she hangs onto a "bucking" lamb for a few seconds before sliding into the dirt. You never know if the kid will get up pumped up with pride or busted up with tears. Thankfully, it is usually the former.

Test Your Nativity

Do you know these important
Coloradans? Match names with
deeds:

1. William Jackson Palmer

2. Charles Boettcher

3. Molly Brown (unsinkable)

4. Temple Buell

5. William Byers

6. Alexander M. Cassidy

7. Adolph Coors

8. Dana Crawford

9. Jack Dempsey

10. John Evans

11. Barney Ford

12. Prinster Brothers

13. John & Charles C. Gates, Jr.

14. Dick & Maddie Gibson

15. Elrey B. Jeppesen

16. Frank P. Marugg

17. Ouray

18. Lawrence Cowle Phipps

19. Paco Sanchez

20. Horace, Augusta & Baby Doe

21. Byron "Whizzer" White

22. Charles and William Bent

23. Clara Brown

a. Supplied mines, dabbled in cement, sugar, insurance and livestock. His foundation helps Colorado projects.

b. Synonymous with rubber, they made the first steel studded tires and a device to defeather chickens.

c. Territorial governor, founder of schools, railroads, and a Fourteener.

d. Taking his dead brother's name Bill became the Manassa Mauler.

e. The Jed Clampett of Colorado, he found oil in 1862 and started Conoco.

f. First woman and African-American member of the Society of Colorado Pioneers.

g. Rhodes scholar and pro football player, better known for sitting on the bench of the Supreme Court.

h. Founder of largest brewery (at one site).

i. Designed the first Cherry Creek Shopping Center and 27 Denver schools.

j. Map maker for the birds; DIA terminal is named for him.

k. Inventors of the Waterpik®, they're better known for their love of jazz.

l. Restauranteur and innkeeper, fought for black suffrage before statehood.

m. Her name is synonymous with the restoration of Denver's LoDo.

n. Founder of Colorado Springs

o. Founder of a Spanish radio station, he built low cost housing and the Museum of Mexican History.

p. In 1831 with Ceran St. Vrain, they built a fort on the US/Mexican border that dominated trade between the two countries.

q. From shipping clerk to the top of Carnegie Steel, he retired a millionaire at age 39 in Denver.

r. The Tabors or Colorado's answer to a real life soap opera.

s. A musician, he invented the auto immobilizer, better known as the Denver Boot.

t. Social outcast, married well, known for her buoyancy.

u. They started the City Market grocery in Grand Junction in the 1920s.

v. 1859 founder of the Rocky Mountain News

w. Linguist and realist. He felt a treaty with the US was like a hunter's pact with a buffalo–after it was shot.

Answers are on the last page.

High-Tale-ing It

While Texans are obsessed about size, for NATIVES it is all about altitude.

- The world's highest road tunnel is the Eisenhower Tunnel on I-70, which crosses the Continental Divide at 11,158 feet. It is also one of the longest road tunnels.
- Alma is the highest town in the US at 10,355 feet, while Leadville is the highest city at 10,188 feet. Colorado requires 2000 in population to be a city.
- The highest suspension bridge in the world is the Royal Gorge by Cañon City. It stands at 1,053 feet above the Arkansas River.
- The highest dead-end, paved road goes to the top of Mt. Evans at 14,270 feet. The highest US paved road is the 48-mile Trail Ridge Road through Rocky Mountain National Park. It peaks at 12,183 feet. (A night trip is best for stargazers.)
- The highest US mountain pass is Mosquito Pass between Leadville and Fairplay at 13,188 feet-unpassable July 4, 2003 because of snow!
- The highest railroad in the US is the Pikes Peak Cog Railway at 14,110 feet.

You get the idea. Here's one to humble a Texan or New Yorker: Denver has America's largest airport at 53 square miles, twice the size of Manhattan.

Would You Believe?

Unless you are into history, you may not know this about the state of Colorado.

You never had to leave Denver's Brown Palace Hotel when it was built in 1892. You could come out at the Annual Debutante Ball, marry, eat, drink, sleep, sneak through a tunnel to the brothel next door and even be cremated in the hotel's basement.

The Otis Elevator Company had their offices in a one-story building.

The Red Comet Fire Extinguisher Company burned down.

In the 1970s non-NATIVES smuggled Coors out of Colorado because it wasn't distributed outside the state. These same people immigrated here and never touch the stuff. Why limit yourself when you have a choice of about 100 breweries and brewpubs across the state? Colorado brews more beer per capita than any other state and Coors brewed over 1 billion gallons in 2003.

The late Israeli prime minister Golda Meir (Myerson) attended high school at North High in Denver.

Three years after the Cripple Creek gold strike in 1891, the Colorado Springs Mining (stock) Exchange traded more shares than any other exchange in the world.

Frank Lloyd Wright lost the bid to design the Air Force Academy in 1954.

A good silver mine is above timberline ten times out of nine.

Denver's Botanic Gardens and the adjacent Cheesman Park were once a massive cemetery. Walter Cheesman controlled the water system, overcharged users and was not popular. His wife bought back the public's affection after his death by donating Cheesman Park, its pavilion and the Governor's mansion. The Boettchers bought the mansion from Mrs. Cheesman and in 1960 turned it over for the governor's use.

The Pioneer Monument in Denver is modeled after Kit Carson.

In Denver the post office only acknowledges two directions–south and east. Thus, it is unnecessary to use the "north" or "west" abbreviations when addressing mail.

Many happenings in *On the Road* by Jack Kerouac took place in the Capitol Hill area of Denver. Kerouac lived in an apartment at Colfax and Lafayette.

The feasibility of the Peace Corps came from a study done by a Colorado State University professor.

The quarry near Marble, Colorado is the source for the Lincoln Memorial and the Tomb of the Unknown Soldier, Parts I and II.

Empire is the hummingbird capital of the world.

Lee Harrison III was the founder of computer animation for television, winning an Emmy in 1972 for his work in Denver on Jim Henson's Muppets.

Elitch Gardens, an amusement park in Denver, began as the source of fresh vegetables for Elitch Palace, a successful restaurant. The gardens were a zoo, a dancing pavilion and then a theatre built in 1890. Douglas Fairbanks was a stage hand there at age 12. John Elitch founded the Denver Athletic Club. His wife Mary carried on Elitch Gardens after his death. Too bad for those of you, who missed seeing the original gardens before it moved to the Platte River valley. The plant-filled, whimsical grounds were as much fun as the rides.

Colorado license plates, first issued in 1908, were numbered consecutively and passed on to family members. Low numbers went to Denver residents and were in high demand. In 1931 license plate number 1 was acquired by Emily Griffith. Ms. Griffith started an adult educational school that still functions. She was murdered in her mountain cabin. Her killer was never found. When the current mountain image was first used on Colorado license plates in the 1960s, it appeared upside down in odd-numbered years.

The Four Mile House built in 1859 is Denver's oldest. It was a stage stop on the Cherokee Trail. Now it is a spot for summer concerts, picnics and tours.

Doc Holiday is buried in Glenwood Springs where he came for relief from tuberculosis.

NATIVE Celebrations

Whether you stay along the Front Range or prefer to take your chances as a gullible traveller at the smaller festivals, there's lots of NATIVE enjoyment to experience throughout the year.

JANUARY: The **National Western Stock Show and Rodeo** is a two-week winter break that attracts half a million people annually. It is authentic western fun. You know it's here if you live downwind of the complex. In Breckenridge there is the **Snow Sculpture Competition**, where teams from around the world carve sculptures from large ice blocks and the **Ullr Festival**, where weird snow Olympians spend a week honoring the Norse god of snow. Greeley celebrates its **Farm Show** with agricultural exhibits. And if you can't give it away, there's the annual **Fruitcake Toss** in Manitou Springs.

FEBRUARY: The **Cardboard Downhill Derby** lets you build a craft out of cardboard and ride down a ski slope. It is very entertaining and during the lull you may ski Arapahoe Basin. Celebrate love during the **Sweetheart City Festival** on Valentine's Day. People come from all over to mail their Valentine cards in Loveland. This is like the April 15th rush to mail income taxes, only a lot more fun. The little known, but greatly appreciated **Jazz on Film Festival** in Denver in mid-month is a great way to experience two media–jazz and film. It's unlikely you'll see this footage elsewhere.

MARCH: The **Denver Pow-Wow** brings together Native Americans from over sixty tribes to dance and drum in full costume.

APRIL: **Spring Splash** is on Winter Park's closing ski day. Skiers dress in goofy costumes and try to ski across a puddle of icy water at the base of the resort. Sort of a solute to polar bears.

MAY: The **Kinetic Sculpture Challenge** near Boulder is like the Cardboard Derby only in teams. The idea is to create a human-powered craft that can go on land, water or mud. May 5th is **Cinco de Mayo**. This is not Mexican Independence Day, (September 16th). It is a celebration of poor Mexican farmers beating the pants off Napoleon's French army in 1862. The French ruled Mexico for three years, but were ousted with U.S. aid. Join the **Hot Time in the Gold Camp** at Cripple Creek, where old-fashioned fire companies have races and start a mouthful of fire with their chili cook-off.

JUNE: This is truly the best people-watching event of the year. The **Capitol Hill People's Fair**, began in 1972 by two churches. There are over 500 booths and stages by crafts people, food vendors and musicians. Expect 250,000 folks. The **Gay PrideFest Parade** comes in a close second in gawking at folks. The **Santa Fe Trail Festival** brings living history, food and fun to Trinidad. **Madame Lou Bunch Day** celebrates the oldest profession in Central City with bed races occupied by madams in period costumes. Glenwood Springs celebrates the **Strawberry Harvest** as it has since 1898.

The **Colorado Renaissance Festival** also begins in June with a 16th century market set up near Larkspur. There are people in period costumes, jousting, jesters and games.

JULY: For a very hot event there's the **Cherry Creek Arts Festival** with over 200 fine art exhibitors and 300,000 visitors. Get there early or melt. Got culture? **Central City Opera House** has been performing most July's since 1932. Participate in the **Burro Days Race** in Fairplay and get your ass over the pass! **Cattleman's Days** give you another chance to see a rodeo with horse races. This has been celebrated since 1900 in Gunnison. **Victor's Gold Rush Days** south of Cripple Creek gives you a chance to do hard-rock mining and ride on the narrow gauge railroad.

AUGUST: Loveland (the city not the ski area) claims the **Sculpture in the Park** is the largest bronze show of its kind in the US with around 150 artists. Tour foundries to see how it is done. The **Colorado State Fair**, another opportunity for Western enthusiasts, is not held in the capitol city, but in Pueblo. For Denverites check out **Western Welcome Week** in Littleton. Do more mining during **Leadville's Boom Days**. Eat yourself silly at the **Peach Festival** in Palisade, the **Sweet Corn Festival** in Olathe or the **Melon Days** at Rocky Ford.

SEPTEMBER: Denver's **Festival of Mountain and Plain**, begun in 1895 and revived in 1983, is like the People's Fair, but with food rather than crafters the main attraction. About 400,000 folks attend over the Labor Day weekend. Over twenty-five of Colorado's wine makers celebrate Winefest at Palisade near Grand Junction. Tall tales can be had in Durango at **Cowboy Days** featuring storytellers and cowboy poets. Take a break from your diet and binge on carbs in Greeley with the **Potato Day Harvest Festival.** Get more culture with the **Telluride Film Festival**.

OCTOBER: Start the month off on a healthy note and go to the **Oatmeal Festival** in Lafayette. The **Denver International Film Festival** gives you a chance to see films before they hit the theaters and query the directors, producers and actors about them. View independent and documentary films, since you may not see them elsewhere. Check the local papers for Halloween "haunts" or visit a ghost town.

NOVEMBER: Take a breather, watch a Bronco game and get ready for the crass commercialism of Christmas. Get in the holiday mood by touring the **Rosemont** in Pueblo. This 37-room mansion, with 85% of its original furnishings, is decorated for the holidays and won't disappoint.

DECEMBER: The **Parade of Lights** takes place at night, so bring something warm in your thermos. Don't miss the lighting of the Denver City and County building. It is the NATIVE thing to do. Make a night of it and see the **Wild Lights** at the Denver Zoo and the **Blossoms of Lights** at the Denver Botanic Gardens. Many mountain towns hold craft bazaars with unique gift-giving ideas for those hard-to-shop-for friends and relatives.

Wrapping It Up

Is that a smile on your face? If so this book did what it was supposed to do and prepared you well enough to pass as a NATIVE. But if your curiosity about Colorado is piqued, then I feel a true sense of accomplishment. We all like to brag about what we know and now you too can blend in better than the NATIVES. Local historical societies can teach you more through special events that bring awareness, fun and something to brag about.

Think of history the way you think of dating–a necessary evil to reach a goal, whether a soul mate or solely knowledge. Like dating we are doomed to repeat our past mistakes until we know more about what is truly important to us.

My sources for creating this book range from living here as a semi-NATIVE for twenty plus years to books, newspapers, on-line data and brochures. Bookstores have travel guides about Colorado, but that is for everyone. To dig deeper, check out the books at the Colorado Historical Society. Libraries and museums in Colorado are also abundantly stocked. Don't forget the out-of-print gems hidden in used and rare book stores. After all if you're going to pass yourself off as a NATIVE, you should know a little bit about the terrain.

Colorado Timeline

1275	Decline of Anasazi due to drought.
1682	LaSalle claims Colorado for France.
1706	Spain claims southeast Colorado.
1776	Escalante & Dominguez trek.
1803	Eastern Colorado comes into US via Louisiana Purchase.
1806	Zebulon Pike explores Colorado.
1821	Southern Colorado comes under Mexican rule. Santa Fe Trail opens.
1828-1838	First fort Ft. Uncompahgre built on Gunnison River. Bent's Fort built for Indian trade in 1834. Other forts, Vasquez, St. Vrain, Lupton and Davy Crockett are also built. Inter-tribal Indian conflicts.
1839	Beaver population declines.
1842	Smallpox epidemic hits Indians.
1844	James Beckwourth settles Ft. Pueblo.
1846	Utes destroy Ft. Uncompaghre.
1848	Army protects first cattle drive. US gets rest of Colorado from war with Mexico. Gold found in California.
1852	Hispanics build first irrigation project in San Luis Valley. Bent builds new fort on Arkansas River.
1852-4	Gunnison, Beale, Heap and Fremont explore for a railroad route through the Rocky Mountains. Utes kill Ft. Pueblo settlers.
1857	First Colorado church is in Conejos.
1858	Denver and Pike's Peak gold rush begins.
1859	Rocky Mountain News is first newspaper. First Texas cattle drive to Colorado. Gold seen near Cripple Creek.
1860	Julesburg is a Pony Express stop.
1861	Colorado Territory is created.
1862	John Evans is governor of territory. Colorado Volunteers burn supplies of Confederate troops at Glorietta Pass, New Mexico. Capitol moves from Colorado City to Golden.
1863	Telegraph reaches Denver. Utes give up San Luis Valley to US.
1864	Chivington kills peaceful Cheyenne at Sand Creek. Georgetown silver rush. As new capitol, Denver finishes Smith Ditch and is flooded by Cherry Creek.

1866	First sugar beets grown in Platte Valley.
1867	Exiling Cheyenne and Arapahoe to Oklahoma ends most conflicts.
1870	Denver gets two railroads after Transcontinental Railroad went through Cheyenne in 1869. Blacks get the vote. State population nears 40,000. Greeley is founded.
1872	First melons grown in Arkansas Valley.
1873	More sheep than cattle are in Colorado. Gold and silver rush begins in San Juans. Ft. Collins and a five year depression begins.
1875	Grasshopper plague ruins farming.
1876	Colorado becomes 38th state.
1877-8	Leadville silver rush begins.
1879	Utes kill Nathan Meeker and are sent to southwest Colorado in 1880-81. First phone comes to Denver.
1880	Population jumps to 194,327. Miners strike in Leadville. Denver is fourth city in the world to use electric street lighting.
1882	US bans Chinese laborers from US.
1883	Fruit growers on Western Slope after Grand Junction gets railroad.
1885-7	Open Range cattle boom ends.
1888	Cliff Palace at Mesa Verde found.
1890	Population is now over 413,000.
1891	Cripple Creek gold rush begins.
1893	US changes to gold standard and causes four year depression. Colorado women get the vote.
1894	State capitol completed. Severe drought in Colorado.
1900-1905	Cheesman Dam is built, state population reaches 539,700 and Great Western Sugar and Holly Sugar are founded.
1906	Mesa Verde National Park is created. State florists ship nationwide.
1908	Denver issues first license plates in US. Capitol dome gets gold leaf.
1909	Colorado becomes most irrigated state (3 million acres).
1910-1	Dearfield begins as black ag colony.
1913	State law requires 8-hour workday in mines, mills and smelters.

1914	Ludlow Massacre occurs when guards burn worker's village during coal strike. Emily Griffith starts Opportunity School in Denver.
1915	Rocky Mountain National Park and Dinosaur National Monument created.
1916	Prohibition hits the state four years prior to the national ban.
1917	Wild West icon Buffalo Bill Cody dies.
1918	Sugar beet industry imports labor from Mexico to replace WWI soldiers.
1921	Arkansas River at Pueblo floods and kills 100. Beginning of KKK power.
1922	First commercial radio license issued.
1928	Moffat tunnel opens at a cost of $18 million and 29 lives.
1929	Cañon City prison riot kills 13.
1932-1938	Eastern Colorado becomes part of Dust Bowl. Southern Utes get back 252,000 acres from the state.
1941-	Wartime building boom begins.
1946	Japanese-Americans sent to Camp Granada. State looses 2700 to WWII.
1947	Dr. Florence Sabin spearheads health reform. Emily Griffith murdered in mountain cabin.
1958	US Air Force Academy opens.
1960s	Environmental concerns grow. 154,208 Coloradans serve and 620 perish in Vietnam.
1976	Big Thompson flood destroys 316 homes, kills 139, costs $35 million. Exxon departs and economy "busts".
1982 1983	Federico Peña becomes first Hispanic Denver mayor. Wellington Webb becomes Denver's
1991	first African-American Mayor. TABOR Amendment allows voters a
1992	say on state and local taxes. Light rail comes to Denver.
1994 1995	Denver International Airport ($4 billion) opens as does Denver's Coors Baseball stadium ($215 million). Broncos win the Superbowl.
1998-99 1999	Denver's Pepsi Center ($160 million) opens for hockey and basketball. New Invesco/Mile High football sta-
2001	dium ($364.2 million) opens.

128

Answers to **Quick Quiz** (page 62):
1.d 2.a 3.d 4.c
5.b 6.d 6.a 8.d

Answers to **Test Your Nativity** (page 114):

1. n
2. a
3. t
4. i
5. v
6. e
7. h
8. m
9. d
10. c
11. l
12. u
13. b
14. k
15. j
16. s
17. w
18. q
19. o
20. r
21. g
22. p
23. f

GRADE SCALE

21-23 = NATIVE
18-20 = Almost NATIVE
16-17 = Semi-NATIVE
13-15 = TRANSPLANT
11-12 = ALIEN
0-10 = Go Back Where
You Came From